Exiled: Stories from Conservative Professors Who Have Been Ridiculed, Ostracized, Marginalized, Demonized, and Frozen Out

Edited by Mary Grabar

Dissident Prof Press
Dissident Prof Education Project, Inc.
P.O. Box 156
Scottdale, GA 30079
www.dissidentprof.com

© 2013 by Mary Grabar

All rights reserved. No part of this book may be reproduced in any form or by any electronic or mechanical means including information storage and retrieval systems without prior written permission from the publisher, except by a reviewer who may quote brief passages in a review. For information contact the publisher.

Cover design by The Biz Wizard, www.thebizwizard.com

This book is dedicated to all scholars who were exiled before they even had a chance.

I would like to thank Professor of Slavic Studies Ewa Thompson for her editorial help on an early draft. Contributor and English Professor M.D. Allen gave a later draft a careful proofreading during the New Year holiday, and other contributors also gave careful readings. Kristina Knutson, my friend, also volunteered her proofreading services. Any mistakes that remain, though, are mine.

I would like to thank Tina Trent for her ongoing editorial help on this and just about every Dissident Prof piece of writing. She is a major organizing and motivational force behind the Dissident Prof Education Project, and a great friend.

Table of Contents

Introduction: The Brain Drain: A Lament for the Loss of Intellectual Capital and the Future of Freedom
   Mary Grabar   1

The Most Sacred Part of Them: Professors Behaving Badly
   M. D. Allen   15

Losing Friends and Dining Alone
   Martin Slann   29

Anti-Anti-Communism and the Academy
   Paul Kengor   37

Stalinism Lite
   Scott Herring   65

"C" for Conservatism, the New Scarlet Letter
   Brian E. Birdnow   73

The Creed of Political Correctness
   Jack Kerwick   83

Afterword: The Formulated Phrase
   Mary Grabar   91

Contributors   109

Introduction: The Brain Drain: A Lament for the Loss of Intellectual Capital and the Future of Freedom

Mary Grabar

This is a collection of stories from colleagues I have met over the years who share some of the same experiences I have had. I worked hard for my Ph.D. in English but now find myself exiled from the status that is accorded these days almost exclusively to radical Leftists.

My experience led me to begin Dissident Prof, dedicated to "Resisting the Re-Education of America," as the motto goes. It's a part of the Dissident Prof Education Project, Inc., a non-profit education reform initiative.

This is a collection of stories from six of my colleagues, most of whom have contributed to Dissident Prof, who were brave enough to write about how the academy has treated them for their heretical ideas—ideas that would have gained them respect and prestige a couple generations ago, indeed, ideas that have withstood the test of time, but that are deemed offensive by the new guardians at the gates of universities. We are dissidents to the reigning ideological orthodoxy on our campuses—supposedly in the land of the free.

This collection is an attempt to make more people aware of what goes on inside the halls of the academy, where traditionalists and scholars who simply ask for openness are denied the opportunity to influence hiring, curricula, textbooks, conferences, and even the chance to interview for a job. The profession that specializes in studying the "marginalized" has no problem marginalizing certain colleagues, specifically by denying careers and respect to those few remaining conservatives and moderates in their midst.

I am continually surprised when I run into conservatives, even politically active conservatives, who are not aware of the situation, who believe that a history professor will even-handedly weigh historical evidence or that an English professor will demonstrate appreciation for a poem, regardless of the author's ethnic characteristics or political affiliation.

I thought such a book as *Exiled* was needed to expose the inner workings of the academy to the public, who may not know, for example, that a historian's curriculum vita is rejected out of hand because the title of his dissertation indicates the historical fact that communists were meeting and planning in a major U.S. city—no matter the careful archival research he has done. It is the same with the literary scholar whose dissertation does not follow the left-wing guidelines for investigating matters that have little to do with literature. Today's specializations, as indicated by a list of prospective incoming graduate students at the university where I work as an adjunct, show that their future students will not be studying the moral stories of Nathaniel Hawthorne, the tragedies, comedies, and sonnets of William Shakespeare, or the metaphysical investigations of romantic and Godly love of John Donne, but the Marxist banalities of gender, post-colonialism, race, and class.

The implications for the future hit me in February 2012 when I came across the posted list of specializations of prospective graduate students. These are the topics as I copied them down: "water," "fat studies," "disability studies," "trauma," "addiction," "voyeurism," and "shell shock." When there was a traditional specialization, like eighteenth- and nineteenth-century British literature, it was paired with something like "disability" and "addiction."

Another mark of the state of affairs: My former English professor at Georgia State University, from whom I took a T.S.

Introduction: The Brain Drain

Eliot seminar, now devotes his scholarship to animals; the disdain he felt for Eliot that I saw in his class in 1993 has now turned to contempt for all poetry or products of human language. He now specializes in interspecies "communication"--part of a growing subspecialty in English departments: "animal studies."

It is no wonder fewer and fewer students are majoring in English. We are in danger of completely losing our literary heritage as those who preserve and transmit the great works are denied the opportunity to do their work. In fact, we are in danger of losing *poetry* itself. For example, although Pablo Neruda was a communist, I felt that his poems should be taught in my world literature courses. The emotions and music of his love poetry were made especially clear when a good friend, who is fluent in Spanish, came and read them to my classes in Spanish, and explained the subtleties of translation. As a traditionalist, I believe that an English class should focus on literary merits first.

In contrast, leftists have conducted a decades-long assault in literary journals on the works of "imperialistic" dead, white European males. They have managed to obliterate the study of those like Milton and Shakespeare to token mentions, and then usually for political sins or secret homosexual leanings and messages. The latter has happened with a conference and then a book on "Shakesqueer." I think I speak for the vast majority of conservative professors who feel that American novelist Willa Cather's lesbianism has little or no bearing on the quality or importance of her novels. The trend of studying her sexuality at the expense of the literary qualities of her writing has been the focus of conservatives' complaints. It's the same for other fields, like history and philosophy.

Even the sciences, once thought to be immune from ideological demands, are being affected. For example, scientists like UCLA epidemiologist James Enstrom whose evidence does not comport with environmentalists' predetermined acceptable levels of particulates get excluded from research projects and even fired.[1] This happens in the social sciences, as well, for example, for the sociologists like University of Texas at Austin professor Mark Regnerus whose study shows that there are some differences in outcome between children of homosexual and heterosexual parents.[2] Such studies are challenged in ways that those that comport with the dominant ideology do not.

The battle for acceptance, for even the airing of research, is constant, as any regular reader of such higher education sites as *Minding the Campus, National Association of Scholars, The Chronicle of Higher Education, Clarion Call, SeeThruEd* and *Inside Higher Education*, will attest. At stake are jobs, degrees, and salaries, as well as the integrity of the academy itself. Especially alarming, as we enter President Barack Obama's second term, is the nationalization of K-12 education through new regulations called Common Core. Common Core's effect on higher education is sure, as "college-ready" standards are lowered, federal tests obviate previous standards, and college entrance exams are modified to reflect new leftist ideological material and abandonment of objective for subjective grading.

Politicians and the public may dismiss the importance of bias in the humanities but will they do so when scientific standards are abandoned to gender equity or environmental *diktats* from the UN? Will they do so when their own lives are at stake as medicine is modified to meet *diktats* of "social justice"? These shifts emerge from the fundamental changes in the humanities. When standards of truth are abandoned in favor of ideology in philosophy, history, and literature, their abandonment in the sciences is just a little ways off, as we see with professors Enstrom and Regnerus. The philosophical shift has begotten a new field called "feminist science" that rejects the scientific method in favor of "women's ways of knowing."[3] We all have a stake in what goes on behind the ivy-covered walls.

I salute dissident colleagues here who have used their security as tenured professors to speak up. A large part of the reason

Introduction: The Brain Drain

we face the situation we are in today, I believe, is because of a failure of nerve on the part of conservative, moderate, and fair-minded liberal professors in the past. When the barbarians, literally brandishing weapons, stormed the gates of academe in the 1960s and early 1970s too many administrators simply capitulated. The stories of cowardice and shameless pandering have been recorded. Scholars are not by nature confrontational, but I have heard about conservative and moderate professors failing to use their influence with even so much as a phone call to situate graduate students or influence hiring decisions. Too often they have cravenly gone along to get along. I myself have watched as professors fail to speak up at meetings where outrageous ideas, like teaching the vile lyrics of rap artist Tupac Shakur as poetry, are proposed. One of the contributors here finds himself in the position I am in, with years put in as an adjunct, and at this point of the game, with nothing to lose except such poorly paying temporary employment. The contributors here all, however, represent the better instincts. Many others who were asked to contribute essays quite logically feared for their livelihoods and declined.

Our first contributor, M.D. Allen, whom I met at a National Association of Scholars conference, delivers his critique in the gentlemanly way that is characteristic of him. I think you will be delighted with his British voice that carries over into his writing. He starts off with the dismal statistics that confirm the trend I was seeing as a graduate student in the 1990s. Back then, the traditionalists were all middle-aged or older. But the new hires uniformly adhered to the radical agenda. It was not difficult to see the future make-up of the department. The commonly accepted ratio of one out of ten professors being conservative is soon to become much, much smaller. A recent study shows what we have known all along: liberal professors and administrators discriminate against conservatives in hiring and promotion.[4]

Allen offers a speech he gave during a colloquium, ironically, on the intersection between professional and personal lives. It relates his experiences, from hearing "trivial," but revealing, comments during meetings, to "sustained and public loutishness." Even his well-intentioned efforts to write about women were met with scathing hostility. Attempts at reconciliation in a "half-dead European male" manner were rejected. Were he not a member of the class to whom "white privilege" belongs, I think Allen might have been the object of much liberal sympathy. Instead, we have the privilege of reading his bemused account of the travails of being the token traditionalist English professor.

Next, Political Science Professor Martin Slann relates his conversion after 9/11 when political correctness emerged from being a mere annoyance to "threaten[ing] to destroy the very norms and values that applaud an individual's freedom." His conference papers on the United Nations, the value of sustaining our Judeo-Christian culture, and the incompatibility of Sharia and political democracy touched some nerves that led to "social rejection." Liberal educators decry "social rejection" as a form of bullying in cases where it concerns those who do not share Slann's support of the West and Israel. Slann finds that eating alone at such conferences is not so bad, though. Perhaps other universities will follow the lead of his, the University of Texas at Tyler, where Slann spends spring recess taking students to Israel.

To criticize Islam in any way or to question the security credentials of anyone who may have ties to the Muslim Brotherhood through family is to open himself to charges of McCarthyism—as indeed has happened after Congresswoman Michele Bachmann asked for a security check on Secretary of State Hillary Clinton's aide Huma Abedin.[5] When former Congressman Allen West called members of the Congressional Progressive Caucus, who were communists or socialists, "communists," he was ridiculed for "Red-Baiting." The way our history is taught, as I know from talking to college freshmen every semester, is that communism was never a real threat to the security of our nation, that it was simply the

Introduction: The Brain Drain

paranoid imaginings of an out-of-control, right-wing senator named Joseph McCarthy. Any attempt to teach the facts about communism (including the excesses of McCarthy as well as the overwhelming number of times he was *right*) is to invite the Alinskyite smearing of one's reputation.

To even do scholarship in this field is to exclude oneself from consideration in the job market, as Grove City College Political Science Professor Paul Kengor, who specializes in Cold War history, shows with an adaptation of his speech, "Anti-Anti-Communism and the Academy." We know that in the English language double negatives cancel each other out, and it is no less true regarding the anti-anti-communists within the academy who deny the horrible realities of communism. Within Professor Kengor's speech is the story of Vladimir Brovkin, Ph.D. in history from Princeton (1984), former associate professor at Harvard, with three published books on the Soviet Union. He is an exile from the Soviet Union and is now an exile from the American academy, thanks to his conniving colleagues. He currently teaches high school in Florida. Read for yourself also Kengor's accounts of reactions from colleagues when he gives presentations and lists the undeniable crimes of communists in world history. (We see a pattern developing here.)

The reaction from students, most of whom have been denied information about this part of history, encouragingly, differs from their elders'. Happily too Kengor has found support at Grove City College where he also directs the Center for Vision and Values. His latest book, *The Communist, Frank Marshall Davis: The Untold Story of Barack Obama's Mentor*, published not by a university press, but by Glenn Beck's imprint, demonstrates how the efforts of the communists in the U.S., beginning in the 1920s, are having their impact today, namely on our president and his advisors.

Kengor has often participated in conferences off college campuses, where he has been forthright about the threat of communism. I became acquainted with his writing through conservative sites on the internet and met him in person when we both made presentations at a Washington, D.C., press conference sponsored by America's Survival, an organization, unlike our current academy, that is not afraid to investigate threats to national survival, like communism.

And speaking of happily, Scott Herring, who has shared dispatches from California, specifically "occupied" UC-Davis, at Dissident Prof, and who resists the label "conservative" (and probably all labels), offers another one of his sketches of the absurd state of academia. He describes his conversion from typical laidback Californian in the early 1990s and his attempts at political correctness in the classroom. But as you shall see, you can never be politically correct enough, even in a class on Literature of the Wilderness. Happily for him too he teaches at a place where students are immersed in the real world (pre-medicine) and where some are from places where communism could not be denied as a "red scare" — Vietnam. Read "Stalinism Lite" to treat yourself to the wry humor of Herring.

Brian Birdnow, who does not have such a happy story in his professional life, however, has persevered, even as he has labored under conditions that would have had social justice advocates howling were he a Chicano lettuce picker. While many agitate for rights and unionization of graduate students and adjuncts, few admit that those who do not adopt the radical agenda are consigned to perpetual adjunct status, teaching more than twice as many classes as the average course load, for wages that work out to be under minimum wage.

It is true that most of the adjuncts are liberals who are not immune to today's shifting academic job market. But I've seen them land full-time positions, while my conservative colleagues had to continue scrabbling for a living as adjuncts. While liberals may blame evil "corporatists" who run universities for such economic inequities, the fact remains that it is faculty senates that have voted for farming out labor-intensive lower-division courses to adjuncts in order to free themselves for research and more interesting, less labor-intensive graduate seminars or upper-division courses.[6]

So Brian Birdnow has found himself working as an adjunct for over 12 years, while he has sent out scores of job applications. He, too, has been punished for having the "wrong ideas," something that becomes evident to hiring committees from the title of his dissertation — *so* provocatively titled — "The St. Louis Five: The Smith Act, Communism and the Federal Courts in Missouri 1952-1958." The mere *investigation* of communism becomes a fraught issue in a day when historians would rather ignore or dismiss that period in favor of light social issues, like cookbooks, essays by junior high school girls, the crisis of American masculinity in the 1950s, and the American medical community's response to masturbation between 1870 and 1920. These were actual thesis and dissertation topics of candidates who competed with Birdnow for a teaching position. His dissertation, published later as a book by the same title, is a detailed study based on original court research, and written in an elegant, evenhanded style. That, and other publications, mattered for little, nor did the student petitions to have him hired full-time, when he was beat out by an Oklahoma State University graduate "whose scholarly output consisted of writing about prostitution in Tulsa."

Philosophy professor Jack Kerwick shares a fate similar to Birdnow's, traveling to three or four campuses to teach ten to twelve courses a year, including summers. While he does not point to one instance of discrimination or hostility, he describes a general state of affairs in the academy, where the conservative does not feel welcomed. Most of our superiors are clever enough to not tip their hand when it comes to giving reasons for not hiring or promoting a conservative. They have legal advice, paid for by the citizens at public universities, for skirting lawsuits. Even in the rare situation, when they become careless, they prevail in discrimination cases.[7] It is much more difficult to prove discrimination on the basis of ideology than race or gender, for obvious reasons. Kerwick observes in his field of philosophy what our first contributor, M.D. Allen, observed in his field of English—that the ruling priestly class has established a new creed. Unlike a religious creed, however, this secular creed's authority emerges from those in power. There is no tradition, sacred text, or even notion of higher authority against which mortals can test their assertions. It simply becomes a creed of the powerful. It is frightening in its arbitrariness.

Not surprisingly, the new dogma was first imposed through campus takeovers, often including weapons and hostage-taking, and always with mobs. This was in the 1960s. The "free speech" movement display of profanity and vulgarism was launched by Mario Savio on the UCLA campus in 1964, and led to over 300 such campus takeovers in the 1960s. Walter Berns, who was teaching at the Cornell campus during the 1969 takeover there, blames then president James Perkins' capitulation to demands to change the course of study under the guise of "black studies" for the succeeding surrenders to "students armed only with epithets ('racists,' 'sexists,' 'elitists,' 'homophobes'), studies of numerous victim groups, speech codes and political correctness, and affirmative action admissions and hiring."[8]

Then, as now, the objective was not diversity—not even ethnic, racial, or gender diversity—but a fundamental change in academic standards. Today, one's status as a member of the protected groups does not provide protection. I know as a conservative woman who has not qualified for scholarships, research funding, or full-time positions—in spite of my immigrant, working class background. There is a clamping down on dissidents on our campuses similar to that in communist countries, like the former Yugoslavia, from which my parents brought me as a two-year-old. The best art that Western civilization has produced has been denigrated and abandoned in favor of violent ghetto doggerel and poetry that is explicitly and deliberately pornographic—and that serves as

Introduction: The Brain Drain

propaganda.⁹ It was witnessing this onslaught that spurred me to investigate conservatism while I was in graduate school. The more I read of the conservative writers my professors disparaged, the more I began to see that true intellectual rigor and literary joy lay with conservatism—the side that values truth and beauty, and seeks to *conserve* "the best which has been thought and said."

We saw a revival of the intimidation strategies of the 1960s during the Occupy Wall Street movements of 2011-2012 on our campuses, but carried to a more sophisticated level, and therefore less discernible to the public. To my dismay, at Harvard University, respected economics professor Gregory Mankiw was attacked and demonized by his colleague, Professor Steven Marglin. His offense? He taught free market principles in his introductory economics class, for which he has also written a bestselling textbook. Marglin used college freshmen to stage a walkout and then held a teach-in denouncing Mankiw's *ideas*. In a case reminiscent of the self-denunciation at Moscow show trials, Mankiw then wrote an op-ed for the *New York Times* in which he applauded protestors, who rudely walked out of his class, for "thinking beyond their own parochial concerns." And at UC-Davis Chancellor Linda Katehi who, quite reasonably, had ordered police to use tear gas on belligerent protesting students, was greeted by angry hordes of students, spurred on by English professor Nathan Brown. The fear on her face in the video of the scene is visible. The outcomes, with the firing of a police officer, due to the demands of the mob, are not encouraging for the future of academia.¹⁰

As conservative speakers know, walkouts and disruptions with noise and physical attacks from students are not uncommon on college campuses. But such a change in attitude arises from a change in scholarship, where intimidation is glorified, and standards of fairness, openness, and genteel comportment are abandoned. Tips for making such institutional changes through infiltration were described in a book by the feminist scholar "Ms. Mentor," who writes a regular column for *The Chronicle of Higher Education*. She offered advice to female academic job seekers about how to fool hiring and tenure committees. That was in the 1980s and 1990s. In 2011/2012, female chancellors and other academics were capitulating to demands of Occupy Wall Street, and, ironically, being intimidated on their very campuses, by young, insubordinate male professors. I do not know if the feminists are struck by the irony of Chancellor Katehi groveling before mobs of students spurred on by a hotheaded Marxist English professor, or by the irony that some of our best universities archive the materials of rappers who glorify the sexual degradation of women. Again, the conservative woman who makes objections will not be appreciated for bringing "gender diversity" to a campus.

And it just struck me in terms of the contents of this collection that I am "differently gendered" from the contributors. (Or, as a student, who was very involved in Occupy Wall Street last year, put it "gender identified.")

But none of these gentlemen contributors would dare do what an overpaid Marxist Critical Theory professor did and rile up students to threaten their female boss. Indeed, I believe these "patriarchs" would respect her authority and decisions for keeping the campus safe. Among such colleagues, I know of some who confront the poseurs who teach on campuses and include pornographic poetry on their vita. Had they been in charge of hiring, they would have welcomed well-qualified women and others to the table. Their standards are as Matthew Arnold put it, simply, "the best which has been thought and said."

But as we have seen, the barbarians have overturned the debate table and taken their demands into the streets, with ignorant students following them. Recent developments, like the support of professors for Occupy Wall Street and the romanticizing of such violent protests in classroom lessons by activist-professors, make it feel as if the 1960s are back. And it was in the 1960s that a second wave of feminism began as the women of the "movement" realized what cavemen the young long-haired revolutionaries were. Will they today? Will they realize the enormity of the threats coming from the revolutionary agenda, like Sharia, the glorification of violence and rape, speech codes, and censorship?

Perhaps they should listen to the six contributors to this collection, all of one race and gender, not surprisingly, who have been frozen out for defending intellectual freedom, high academic standards, and Western civilization.

---

[1] "ACLJ Files Suit Against UCLA After Professor Is Fired for Blowing Whistle on Junk Science." ACLJ.org. June 14, 2012.

http://aclj.org/free-speech-2/lawsuit-against-ucla-after-professor-fired-for-blowing-whistle-on-junk-science

[2] Kolowich, Steve. "Is the Research All Right?" *Inside Higher Ed.* July 13, 2012.

http://www.insidehighered.207elmp01.blackmesh.com/news/2012/07/13/ut-austin-scrutinizes-ethics-controversial-same-sex-parenting-study

[3] "Feminist Epistemology and the Philosophy of Science." *Stanford Encyclopedia of Philosophy.* March 16, 2011.

http://plato.stanford.edu/entries/feminism-epistemology/

[4] Smith, Emily Esfahani. "Survey shocker: liberal profs admit they'd discriminate against conservatives in hiring, advancement." *The Washington Times.* August 1, 2012.

http://www.washingtontimes.com/news/2012/aug/1/liberal-majority-on-campus-yes-were-biased/?page=1

[5] Kincaid, Cliff. "Where is Huma Abedin's Security Clearance Form?" *Accuracy in Media.* July 31, 2012.

http://www.aim.org/aim-column/where-is-huma-abedins-security-clearance-form/

[6] Bousquet, Marc and Cary Nelson. *How the University Works: Higher Education and Low-Wage Nation.* New York; New York University Press, 2008.

[7] Jacobson, William A. "College faculty applicant wins but loses discrimination lawsuit against U. Iowa Law School. *College Insurrection.* November 24, 2012.

http://collegeinsurrection.com/2012/11/conservative-faculty-applicant-wins-but-loses-discrimination-lawsuit-against-u-iowa-law-school/

[8] Berns, Walter. "The Assault on Universities: Then and Now." In *Reassessing the Sixties* (New York, W.W. Norton), 1997. 163.

[9] Grabar, Mary. "The Porno Prof at Hamilton." *Minding the Campus.* August 31, 2011.

http://www.mindingthecampus.com/forum/2011/08/the_porno_prof_at_hamilton.html

[10] Scott Herring wrote a post for Dissident Prof on the faux outrage over the "abuse" of students with pepper spray that was less potent than what experienced hikers test before they go out into bear-country.

Herring, Scott. "The Pepper Spray Task Force Report: Ginning Up Outrage for Fun and Initiatives at UC-Davis." *Dissident Prof.* April 16, 2012.

http://www.dissidentprof.com/home/102-the-pepper-spray-task-force-report

The Most Sacred Part of Them: **Professors Behaving Badly**

M. D. Allen

On 4 July, 2012, John M. Ellis and Charles L. Geshekter published an article that chronicles the descent of academia into partisan corruption. "Democrats Dominate UC and CSU Faculties" charts the decline of California's state universities from 1969, when there were five Democrats to three Republicans teaching on the publicly-funded campuses of the University of California and California State University, and charts it not merely to the present day (when the ratios are effectively 18:1 in the humanities, 21:1 in the social sciences, and 10:1 "even in the apolitical natural sciences") but to tomorrow, or the day after tomorrow, when the disparity will be something like *64:1*. Ellis and Geshekter justify this last figure by examining the political imbalance in the three highest academic ranks: Democrat full professors, those academics nearest to retirement, presently outnumber Republicans 8.3:1; the figures for associate professors, the next rank down, are 30:1; but those for assistant professors, nearly all of whom have been hired over the last six years and who have three decades or more of influence on university teaching and research ahead of them, are the astonishing ones I have chosen to italicize above.

And I'm going to italicize them again. *Sixty-four to one!* How can such numbers come to be in a country where people self-identify as conservative rather than liberal at the rate of two to one? Let me tell you how they come to be. They are the result of a decades-long power-grab on the part of the academic Left, an assault motivated by intellectual and moral conceit and largely unrestrained by professional or personal scruple.

For the past twenty-two years I have taught at one of the University of Wisconsin Colleges, that is, at one of the thirteen two-year campuses scattered across the state that together constitute a unit of the UW System. Every year the UW Colleges hold a "Colloquium" at which issues of alleged professional importance are discussed. In 2007 the topic was the intersection between our professional and private lives. A colleague on the Colloquium's organizing committee who had heard a couple of my occasional animadversions on the ubiquity of leftist bias in the academy invited me to participate. I gave the talk that follows. It is an account of professors behaving badly due to political predisposition, and the examples range from the relatively trivial, although revealing, like interrupting a committee meeting with delighted praise of President Clinton, to acts characterized by sustained and public loutishness. (I have edited the talk very lightly to clarify some references for readers who do not work in universities.)

The Leftist Tilt and the Isolated Conservative, delivered 24 May, 2007

It's 1993. I've been in the US for three or four years but I've spent the dozen or so years before that entirely elsewhere, first in England writing my dissertation, then teaching in the Middle East. So I'm seriously out of the loop. Furthermore, I've had my head down since my arrival in Wisconsin, working hard, trying to do all the things one has to do to get tenure. I'm aware of the so-called Culture Wars but only peripherally, and they don't seem to impinge on my life. I am not unsympathetic to the Left's position in some matters, insofar as I know and understand it. Take the canon, of some importance to those of us who teach in an English Department. Human nature being what it is, I think it very likely that the contributions of women and minorities have been undervalued. Also, I think I may be able to make use of this new focus of interest: I know a little about Western attitudes to the Arab world and Arab attitudes to the West. Maybe this can be another string to my bow. I am not, of course, suggesting that anybody else has ever espoused multiculturalism for career reasons. I am only talking about my coarse-grained self.

So when an annual literary conference held at the University of West Virginia chooses "Cross-Cultural Encounters" as its theme, I hopefully submit an abstract entitled "The New Path: English Women Travelers in the Middle East." I'm doubly pleased when the conference organizer not only accepts the paper but asks me to be a plenary luncheon speaker. I'm told to expect a diverse audience: conference members assembled at the final Sunday luncheon but also faculty spouses and members of the local community. In fact, on Friday night the big-name scholar who is scheduled to speak immediately before the "banquet" takes the wrong motorway exit and I agree to fill the gap. These relatively formal circumstances perhaps exacerbate the contrast between what at least some of those attending the conference expect and what I have to offer. I assume a light tone, provide a general overview of my topic, and tell a few mildly amusing stories about the adventurous women I am discussing. The reaction takes me aback. Incredulity seems to be its first constituent element, something not very far from rage its second. I am perceived by many of the women academics there as patronizing them, the travelers, and feminist studies generally. Despite what I regard as a sympathetic and not disrespectful attitude, it is made clear to me in what the conference organizer would later call a "spirited" question-and-answer session that my paper is not, or not merely, inadequate (ill informed, unscholarly) but "offensive," and that I am not, or not merely, intellectually lacking but gravely morally at fault. I am a pariah from Friday night to Sunday afternoon. When I finally get into the little plane that takes me out of Morgantown, West Virginia, I sigh with relief.

Incidentally, twelve years later the President of what is now apparently the best university in the world loses his job in part because he wonders out loud whether all differences between the sexes are due to socialization. Larry Summers, President of Harvard, suggests that "innate differences" between the sexes might help explain why, for example, only twenty per cent of professors in science and engineering are women. Despite assuring his audience that "I'd like to be proven wrong on this one," his remarks cause deep anger. Professor Nancy Hopkins of MIT walks out and claims "I would've either blacked out or thrown up" if she hadn't, a response that immediately takes me back to the self-righteous huffing and puffing of West Virginia.

It's either 1999 or 2000, I can't remember. But the point of my story is that it is the fourth year of President Clinton's second term of office. A certain committee on which I am serving is trying to decide whether certain rules and regulations permit the election or appointment of a certain person to a certain position. With regret, the virtues and talents of this person being what they are, we're coming to the conclusion that they do not. One committee member says, "I wish I could vote for Clinton again!" Almost the entire committee roars with approving laughter, so loud and so prolonged that I almost miss the only intelligible reply. Almost but not quite. I can just about hear another committee member say, "O-h-h-h-h-h, so-o-o-o-o- do I-I-I-I!" Renewed laughter.

It is 2002. UWFox puts on a performance of *The Vagina Monologues*. The choice seems to me unfortunate, the *Monologues* having attained notoriety, among other reasons, for a scene that portrays favorably alcohol-facilitated child-rape at the hands of a cynical adult lesbian, but I'm not in the business of censorship. A panel discussion is organized. I am one of the two "conservative" speakers, along with a colleague from UWFox's Art Department. The pro-*Monologues* speakers are the play's producer or director or whatever she is and the boss of the local women's shelter. I have met the latter socially. As I know how to behave, I approach her just before the discussion begins and pleasantly remind her of the occasion. She thinks for a minute, remembers, and makes a quick acknowledgment. From beginning to end of this admittedly brief exchange she does not look me in the face.

There is so much local interest in the panel, so many more people attend than were anticipated, that we all have to move from the assigned room to a lecture hall. The actresses enter as a group, joking and laughing, triumphant and cocky. One of them learns that my colleague is an ad hoc in his department. With reference to that status, she cheerfully says, "It shouldn't be difficult to make him look a fool!" Laughter. When my fellow conservative and I speak we are interrupted from the floor. The actresses laugh scornfully, roll their eyes, nudge their neighbors. I am hissed as I speak.

At the end of the panel, I go to the office of the play's director, partly in the interests of maintaining collegiality, believe it or not, and partly because this is my gentlemanly and delicate Half-Dead European White Male way of offering her a painless way of expressing regret at the protracted shamefulness of the scene that has just occurred. I would have been content with very little, something along the lines of, "Well, Malcolm, you and I are never going to agree about anything politically but I'm sorry that that happened." She cannot understand why I am there. Still pumped, and with a fixed half-smile on her face, she waits for the Village Idiot to leave. When I see that, I leave. Within a couple of minutes she is in the open corridor, sneering about the treatment just meted out to me ("Malcolm wasn't very popular, was he?"). This is not the situation I had suffered from at the University of West Virginia, which was a spontaneous and enraged attempt to teach me a lesson. This is an organized and *premeditated* attempt publicly to humiliate into silence an unfashionable view. It is an attack on free speech, and it would not be tolerated if the gender or ideological shoe were on the other foot. The fact that I do *not* find in my In-box within the hour a general e-mail from UWFox's Dean and CEO condemning what has happened and offering support; the fact that, despite the considerable non-campus presence, I do *not* read in the local paper a letter from the same person assuring the people of the Fox Valley that UWFox remains committed to civility and freedom of speech; the fact that the untenured producer of the *Monologues* does *not* find the social pressure to apologize irresistible, that, in fact, there is no such pressure at all, but that rather, in the topsy-turvy world of academia, I, the person who protests against public loutishness from the Left, am myself accused of attacking free speech — all of this makes me think that an exceptionally severe critic might conceivably find a certain imperfect consistency of moral stance at the University of Wisconsin-Fox Valley. I silently decide that I shall abandon my previous plan of naming any future child I may have "Fox Allen."

It is 2006. As a member of the Madison Chapter of the Dickens Fellowship, I am attending the Annual Birthday Luncheon. The Dickens Fellowship is a group of amateur enthusiasts with a sprinkling of academics. Every year we have a lunch followed by a speaker from outside the group. This year the speaker is a member of the English Department at UW-Whitewater. He elects to talk about the novel we have been discussing, *Barnaby Rudge.* His procedure is to take various characters in the novel and insultingly compare them with members of the Bush administration. So Dennis the hangman, for example, is Dick Cheney. Barnaby himself, *of course*, is President Bush. Note to non-English majors: Barnaby is technically an idiot, Educationally Sub-Normal, whatever the latest euphemism may be. All this seems to me gratuitous, rather sophomoric. But there is more. There are illustrations, projected on to a screen. They show Republican politicians in postures of degradation. Condoleezza Rice especially incurs the speaker's contempt. She is a woman and an African

American but she is a Republican too. The speaker makes comments about her as a single woman that I am not going to repeat. One of the illustrations shows her dressed as a dominatrix. She is standing in a little chariot, whipping forward Dick Cheney, who is dressed in bondage gear and harnessed to it. I wait until the Q&A and then, for the first time ever, I think, lose my temper in public. I remember using the phrase "grossly and stupidly insulting," then I walk out. Just for once I do myself a bit of good, and get a few letters and e-mails of support over the next week.

I could go on. I have had to select ferociously in an effort to keep within my time. But the point is made. T. E. Lawrence, who helped coordinate a nationalist revolt against an imperial power, wrote that the English have been independent for so long that the sense of national freedom is like the saliva in our mouths: it's tasteless. Let me borrow his simile for very different purposes and say that in the present-day academy the ubiquity and moral correctness of leftist attitudes and beliefs amongst people who consider themselves intelligent are like the saliva in your mouths. It is not my purpose here to ask how this came about but it is so. Correspondingly, the stupidity and evil of non-leftist positions are self-evident. My colleagues, I believe, almost never hear the conservative viewpoint from an academic, and I hope you're all noticing the delicate scrupulosity of that "almost." From Uncle Herman at a Summer barbeque, perhaps, from the woman who does your hair or the man who fixes your AC, perhaps. From a colleague, almost never. When you do hear it some of you take personal offense. Allen's Law (as doubtless it will very soon be internationally known) states, "In academia the mere utterance of conservative views in and of itself will cause pain or anger." Dissent will either be made dangerous with malice aforethought ("It shouldn't be difficult to make him look a fool!") or it will cause distress on those rare occasions it does crop up. This sort of bigotry can manifest itself at any time in any situation, but, as I'm supposed to be talking about the intersections of professional and private lives, I'm now working my way round to our social lives.

We all have the sort of job that overlaps with what we would be doing for pleasure if we did not have to work. We spend more than the regular forty hours a week "working," and, indeed, for most of us, the distinction between work and pleasure is blurred. Academics tend to spend their free time with other academics because they don't know anybody else. The last dinner party I went to consisted of six people: three university professors, two people who work in or attached to a university in non-pedagogical roles, and a former high school teacher. We hadn't even got to the table before the anti-Bush jokes started, and I don't mean Leno/Letterman jokes we can all laugh at about presidential inarticulacy. I mean venomous and despication-fuelled jeers that create a "chilly climate," as the feminists would say, for those of us who do not hate President Bush with the sort of hatred you would normally reserve for the person who kidnapped and repeatedly raped one of your children.

In conclusion, I am aware of the possibility of giving an apparently exaggerated account of the consequences of being openly conservative in the academy. It is, of course, the case that one's views are occasionally received with courtesy even by those who strongly disagree with them. However, my point remains. If one does not subscribe to the prevailing assumptions and beliefs then one is living in enemy territory. There are so few conservatives teaching in higher education first because they are relentlessly kept out and secondly because if by a miracle one does get tenure he is treated like dirt. As, perhaps, I am now about to discover again.

*   *   *

So that was the end of my speech. There followed courteously phrased, if wary, questions. After that I had a line of people who wanted to thank me and shake hands, the first — and, to date, the last — time this has ever happened to me. My first thought was that the line boded well for the future of my profession; my second, rooted in the perception that the questioners seemed largely tenured or tenure-track Ph.D. holders and the hand-shakers untenured or relatively low-level functionaries, was less optimistic. Here was a reflection of a class divide I may possibly have observed in academia on other occasions.

The third of the examples in the 2007 speech that I reproduce above deals with the panel discussion of *The Vagina Monologues*, an event that happened on my own campus, UW-Fox Valley, located in Menasha, about a hundred miles north-east of the state capital, Madison. With a population of 222,000 the "Fox Cities" (Menasha is one of the seven) constitute the third largest conurbation in Wisconsin, after Milwaukee and Madison, and I am by no means suggesting that my neighbors have hay seeds in their hair. It is, however, the case that UWFox is effectively an open-admissions campus, a "teaching institution" that grants a two-year "associate" undergraduate degree. It says something about conditions prevailing in the academy that the sort of behavior I describe above can happen, and its begetter flourish (the faculty member directly responsible was tenured with hardly a hiccup a few years later), not at the UC and CSU campuses discussed by Professors Ellis and Geshekter, nor at UW-Madison, a flagship research institution with a long-standing reputation for liberal politics, but at a small campus in east-central Wisconsin that even some of the locals would be hard pressed to identify with confidence.

But let us move from flyover country to a rather more prominent, and recent, example of the academic Left in action. The Naomi Schaefer Riley affair has been so widely reported and discussed that a brief summary will probably suffice. On 12 April, 2012, *The Chronicle of Higher Education*, the trade newspaper for those teaching and working in higher education, published an article entitled "Black Studies:

'Swaggering Into the Future'" by Stacey Patton. It included a sidebar giving brief details of the dissertations of the "5 Up-and-Coming Ph.D. Candidates" featured. Riley responded with a 500-word post in the *Chronicle*'s "Brainstorm" blog attacking the students' work as "obscure at best and 'a collection of left-wing victimization claptrap,' at worst."

The reaction to her blog, she later wrote, "ranged from puerile to vitriolic," one fellow blogger and many of the commentators predictably condemning her post as "racist," a professor of English and feminist theory composing silly doggerel about Riley, and, again predictably, a host on MSNBC "spew[ing] a four-minute rant." Eventually, 6,500 — *six thousand five hundred* — academics signed a petition demanding that Riley be dismissed. She was. The *Chronicle*'s editor, Liz McMillen, held out for a few days then, to her eternal shame, caved. I take the above details from the first half of Riley's *Wall Street Journal* article "Naomi Schaefer Riley: The Academic Mob Rules" (8 May, 2012). The second half gives an account of her qualifications to write about education, which include two books, and a quick résumé of the work of distinguished scholars who have also expressed misgivings about the academic rigor of Black Studies courses.

Mark Bauerlein, author of *The Dumbest Generation* (2008) and often an acute critic of contemporary education, wrote at least three articles about the Riley affair. In the first, "Naomi Riley and Her Respondents" (4 May, 2012), he notes the "disproportionate nature" of the responses, quoting examples like "cowardly, uninformed, irresponsible, repugnant, and contrary to the mission of higher education" and "breathtaking arrogance and gutless anti-intellectualism," noting too the "scores of insults" in the comments sections. His final paragraph suggests as cause of the "hyper-emotional tenor" the involvement of Black Studies' faculty and students in a world where "Jim Crow, the assassination of MLK . . . , Republican Party politics, and several other tense historical and contemporary off-campus circumstances" make "academic debate with critics impossible." In "Insecurity in Academia" (15 May, 2012), he notes "The voluminousness, the ferocity, the unrestrained vitriol, the emotionalism" of Riley's critics and this time ascribes it in part to the closed nature of academia, where "stated opinions implicate not just others' opinions but their professional standing, ...people's livelihoods." Thirdly, in "The Context of the Riley Affair" (24 May, 2012), he cites the "parochialism" of the academy, quoting a friend who claimed that "To the liberal intelligentsia and many smart liberal politicians, the university is an **asset**, and they desperately want to hold on to it. They get jobs there and they promote the right ideas and research there." When Bauerlein reasonably pointed out that a few conservatives could change nothing about the academy, the friend replied that liberals "worry that the acceptance of one conservative voice opens the door to two, and three, and four. If one of them really belongs there, then the campus is no longer one side's asset."

I find these three explanations (they are not, of course, mutually exclusive but overlapping) cogent. They throw light on my own experiences over the twenty years or so since I first came an unversed and naïve cropper presenting a paper at the University of West Virginia. Yes, of course, Black Studies and the other "Studies" courses and the people who teach and take them are acutely and self-righteously aware of contemporary events and old horrors and injustices. Yes, of course, peer-review and other expressions of professional opinion help make or mar reputations and careers, and all academics know it all the time. And yes, of course, those on the Left assume that the academy is their own preserve and respond with distress (if you're lucky) or defensive anger (if you're less so) to anybody who would seem to threaten that very proper state of affairs. But I would like to suggest a *raison d'être* for venomous leftist rage that goes a little deeper than the reasons proffered by the distinguished Professor Bauerlein.

When my colleagues on the Left bushwhack then ostracize someone at a conference they do not consider they are behaving badly. When my colleagues on the Left implement, if I may quote a phrase from my talk, an "organized and *premeditated* attempt publicly to humiliate into silence an unfashionable view" they do not consider they are behaving badly. When, to continue with my own experiences, they publicly call me a "fool," or send me an obscenely-worded e-mail ("I don't care what you think. Fuck off"), or weep at me ("You have reopened my wounds"), or melodramatically twist their faces into an expression of disgust and contempt when they see me approaching in the corridor, or conspicuously turn their back on me in the faculty workroom and slowly wave to and fro a sheet of paper to waft away the stink of my presence, then they are not behaving badly. By definition, they are on the side of the angels, and, equally by definition, I, who think differently am..., well, on the other side. The very idea of reasoned debate or scholarly colloquy with conservatives is anathema to many academic Leftists, who demand a world free of "racism," and "sexism," and "homophobia," and "greed," as defined by them, although not, perhaps, a world entirely free of delicate self-approbation, or visceral contempt for Christians and Republicans and opponents of homosexual "marriage," much less free of intellectual and spiritual arrogance.

Let us try to be charitable. The wish, indeed the longing, for a pain-free world is not in and of itself condemnable. It is, of course, deep in all of us and constitutes part of a powerful drive that often takes a religious form (at first I wrote "the wish for a *sin*-free world"). However, many — not all — on the Left are secularist, agnostic, or atheist, sometimes aggressively so. For them, there is no future state in which the inevitable tears of this world will be wiped away. This is the only world there is and it therefore matters supremely. They would never express themselves in these terms but when they are opposed, or merely contradicted, *they think the most sacred part of them is under attack* and respond accordingly. Their fear is not, or not primarily, that the prospective thirty years of tenured safety in the Black Studies Department, or the Black Studies Department itself, may be at risk; their fear is that Evil will triumph, and triumph, in their terms, forever. Their fear is not, or not primarily, that funding for the Women's Studies Certificate, or the Women's Studies Department itself, may be at risk; their fear is that Evil will triumph, and, in their terms, will do so forever. The ruthless impetus to exclude conservatives from the academy, and often to insult and degrade any who do get in and so far forget themselves as to voice their opinions is, at root, a debased form of religion.

Not that that means we have to put up with it.

Bauerlein, Mark. "Naomi Riley and Her Respondents." Brainstorm: Ideas and Culture. *The Chronicle of Higher Education.* 4 May, 2012. http://chronicle.com/blogs/brainstorm/naomi-riley-and-her-respondents/46496

-----. "Insecurity in Academia." Brainstorm: Ideas and Culture. *The Chronicle of Higher Education,*15 May, 2012. http://chronicle.com/blogs/brainstorm/insecurity-in-academia/46864

-----. "The Context of the Riley Affair." Brainstorm: Ideas and Culture. *The Chronicle of Higher Education,* 24 May, 2012 http://chronicle.com/blogs/brainstorm/insecurity-in-academia/46864

Ellis, John M. and Charles L. Geshekter. "Democrats Dominate UC and CSU Faculties." *San Jose Mercury News*, 4 July 2012. http://chronicle.com/blogs/brainstorm/insecurity-in-academia/46864

Riley, Naomi Schaefer. "The Most Persuasive Case for Eliminating Black Studies? Just Read the Dissertations." Brainstorm: Ideas and Culture. *The Chronicle of Higher Education*, 30 April, 2012.
http://chronicle.com/blogs/brainstorm/insecurity-in-academia/46864

-----. "Naomi Schaefer Riley: The Academic Mob Rules." *Wall Street Journal.* 8 May, 2012. http://chronicle.com/blogs/brainstorm/insecurity-in-academia/46864

Losing Friends and Dining Alone

Martin Slann

My life story isn't terribly interesting, probably because of a long academic career. In recent years, though, I found myself – a lifelong Democrat – becoming increasingly disenchanted with the party that my family had endorsed for three generations since at least the time of the New Deal. What was happening to me? As a political scientist, it was rare to encounter anyone who revealed him or herself as a Republican, though I did suspect there was an occasional instructor who remained in the closet. I spent three pleasant decades on one campus and, through that time, encountered precisely two colleagues in my department who enthusiastically identified themselves as Republicans. Both became really close friends and I have fond memories of the times and debates we enjoyed together. I always laughed when they tried to persuade me that the Democrat party was moving more and more toward the looney and totalitarian left. I voted for McGovern without enthusiasm, for Carter (before learning he was an anti-Semite), for Mondale (but don't remember why), and for Dukakis mainly because he took public transportation to work when he was governor of Massachusetts. And yes, I voted for Clinton twice. True, he was (and certainly remains) a narcissist who had the morals of a rabbit, but at least it was possible to persuade myself that he was an ideological centrist. Relatively speaking he was, probably. But even the center of the Democrat party seemed to be moving relentlessly to the radical left. Finally, I voted for Gore in 2000 before learning just how green he really was and wanted us to be.

That was the end. Over time, I had become a raving moderate and found the policies advocated by the Democratic party to be, well, economically and socially destructive. In 2004 the break became complete: I voted for George W. Bush, experienced no regret, suffered no anguish, and had no remorse. At the time, I held an administrative position at the Penn State campus in Wilkes-Barre. People there worked tirelessly for the Kerry campaign, were annoyed with Bush for being dumb and starting wars in Iraq and Afghanistan for no good reason, and genuinely believed Dick Cheney was the devil incarnate. They could not understand how I could believe anything else. Their confusion was reasonable. Soon after arriving on campus, I started a Model United Nations student organization and helped prepare its members to represent a country at a regional conference. By this time I had come to the conclusion that the real United Nations was essentially controlled by thugs who represented governments that happily engaged in genocidal activities against their own people. Libya then chaired the Human Rights Council. Upon hearing that, I could only say "What!" The world for me had become something silly. The Human Rights Council's public face was a regime that never in four decades held a free election, frequently murdered real or perceived opponents, and was headed up by a deranged colonel who drank warm camel milk each morning in his tent and who another Arab dictator had proclaimed was "crazy."

Something else was going on. After 9/11, I observed a tendency that was both disconcerting and somewhat scary. Most Democrats and many Republicans knocked themselves out to assure the American people that Islam is a peaceful religion that had been "hijacked" by violent radicals. Even more telling, this was the same line being offered in thousands of classrooms by members of the liberal academic establishment. And it got worse. A lot of colleagues in the social sciences began suggesting to their students that the deaths of 3000 Americans were essentially our own fault. We had provoked the terror that was now being visited upon us by our arrogance, our refusal to "rein in" Israeli aggression and occupation of so-called Palestinian territory, our support of authoritarian governments, and, finally, our refusal to consult with our "European allies." It did not seem to matter to critics of American foreign policy that the United States had been attacked by genocidal sociopaths who were carrying on a fourteen-hundred-year war against the West, democracy, the free market, and the Judeo-Christian tradition of human dignity and individual rights.

This was a conflict that began well before 9/11 and well before the establishment of Israel in 1948. A doctrine of moral parity evolved that condemned the notion that the West is the Best. It insisted that a religious ideology – Islam – that encourages and approves of mutilation, rape, forced conversion, supremacism over all other faiths, and the elimination of Western civilization should be treated with respect and deference as at least a co-equal to Western culture. Multi-culturalism and political correctness had always been annoying, but now they threatened to destroy the very norms and values that applaud an individual's freedom to pursue her or his own destiny that I had assumed, correctly, really were superior to any other.

The insinuation of Sharia law into American jurisprudence was the last straw. Or perhaps the last straw had to do with clowns such as Imam Rauf and his wife, Daisy Khan (of 9/11 mosque fame), stating that there is no real contradiction between the United States Constitution and Sharia law. Thank goodness for the clarification. I was seriously worried that the recommended public beheadings for adultery and apostasy just might violate some obscure constitutional amendment. What a relief.

To be fair, the Pew organization conducted a multi-nation study a few years ago and discovered that only 7 percent of Muslims were willing to do violent things in order to establish Sharia law. (Another fourth would be supportive but not dirty their hands themselves.) This low proportion is frequently cited by Muslims and apologists as remarkably minimal and, obviously, it would certainly be easy to discover that 7 percent of Buddhists, Christians, Hindus, and Jews were also willing to kill millions to make the world safe for their form of fanaticism. Actually, it wouldn't because they don't. And 7 percent of the global Islamic population is over 110 million people, or the equivalent of four Afghanistans under the Taliban.

I at long last determined to go public with my transformation into a conservative, Islamophobic, and the West-really-is-better-than-the-rest ghoul. Over the last few years, I have given presentations at several regional political science and international studies conferences about the moral bankruptcy of the United Nations (and a corollary plea for the United States to leave it) and the argument that there is no hope of ever making Islam and Sharia compatible with political democracy. The presentations were all rather predictably received with hostility and anger. Members of the audience — mostly fellow academics — groaned and sighed throughout the presentations. Panel discussants expressed their disgust with my arguments. On some occasions, several members of the audience vehemently insisted that they were "offended." One person, to really make the point, stated that he was "offended and . . . offended." He sputtered and was visibly upset.

The debate went downhill from that point. Of the fifty or so people in the room, no one suggested that some of the points I was making — that the Bill of Rights really would not get very far in an Islamic society and that Sharia law should not get very far in ours — might be considered. The kindest word I received was that my comments were "provocative." My responses to the hysterical outbursts only made matters worse. I made a reference to the "so-called Palestinians," initiating one last vehement outburst that the Palestinians really do exist and that they are really oppressed. I agreed that they were oppressed, but by their own governments. The time allotted for the panel mercifully came to an end at that point. I gathered my papers and walked briskly to the elevator for the security and quiet of my hotel room. Happily, no one wanted anything further to do with me. I dined alone that evening, but took solace in the fact that the two glasses of wine I enjoyed were probably better dinner company than any of the offended people in the audience.

At another conference a few months later, I shared a panel with old friends whose expertise was on the United Nations. Their presentations provided a useful summary of the many valuable agencies and activities associated with the UN. Mine focused on how the UN blunted and destroyed hopes for political democracy by refusing to acknowledge that there are some cultures that are destructive of any hope of genuine democratization. These panelists did actually include me in their dinner plans, but they obviously had not read my paper beforehand and could not find any persuasive reason to somehow get rid of me. The food was good, but there was a noticeable tension that became more evident after a couple bottles of wine were consumed, the conversation turned to domestic politics, and former President Bush was condemned for warmongering and threatening Iran instead of engaging its "moderate" leadership. My response was simply that the Obama administration policies were moronic and had made a bad situation much worse. We all decided to skip dessert and depart for our various hotels.

In the fall of 2010, I was invited to present at a conference on the Middle East in Greenville, South Carolina, the following March on any topic of my choosing. I chose Israel since I had visited there numerous times and authored previous papers on the Israeli-Palestinian conflict. Other presentations were, I thought, quite reasonable. The two I sat through provided a modern history of the Middle East while another, delivered by an Islamic scholar, included a lesson on how to formulate a fatwa. When my turn came I simply discussed the politics, demographics, and overall situation of the conflict. I included an explanation of Israel as the only democracy in the region, of the Palestinians whose desire to destroy Israel was many times greater than the one to make peace with it, and the observation by the late foreign minister of Israel, Abba Eban, who correctly pointed out that "the Palestinians will never miss an opportunity to miss an opportunity."

The luncheon that followed enabled me to appreciate how well my comments had gone over. At a table for eight I sat with two friends who had come to hear the presentations. All of the other tables were crowded and all of the other diners completely ignored us. At least this time, I didn't have to eat alone. I did try to engage in conversation with another presenter who simply glared at me. This was a pity since I thought what he had to say about Arabs and Islam was interesting. And one of the two friends mentioned how appalled at my remarks the woman was who sat in front of her. What had I said? Probably nothing more than the fact that Israeli Arabs lived better and enjoyed more individual freedom than any of those in the 22 Arab states that regularly condemn the "Zionist entity" and that Israeli Arabs serve in the parliament, sit on the Supreme Court, and occasionally enter the Miss Universe pageant as Miss Israel. Needless to say, I was not invited to return to the next annual Middle East conference in Greenville or even informed about the dates it was scheduled to occur.

Through all of this, I've learned that some academics are ideological and political bigots. That realization didn't bother me as much as the thought that each of these same people are teaching hundreds of students each year to embrace a grotesque combination of Islam, Marxism, and contempt for democratic values. Some of them will do this for decades to come. Such people don't mellow out. Terrorists from Khalid Sheikh Mohamad to Bill Ayers have indicated that their only regret is not murdering more innocent people. It's all very depressing, but the reception my presentations received convinced me that the good fight is never easy. I've recently revised a textbook I use in my introductory politics classes. I've updated a lot of the material and compare the totalitarian aspects of Islamism with fascism and communism throughout the manuscript. After all, I can also teach hundreds of students a year.

Anti-Anti-Communism and the Academy

Paul Kengor

"Academics consider anti-communism and anti-communists to be vulgar and simple-minded. There are very few communists [among academics], but many, many anti-anti-communists."

—*Richard Pipes, Professor Emeritus, Russian History, Harvard University*[1]

There was no greater threat to faith and freedom worldwide over the last 100 years than communism. There is no disputing that reality. And yet, the failure to teach that essential truth—essential because of the unprecedented destructiveness of that very real communist threat—is itself an affront. Sadly, there are few greater failures in modern academia.

As Mikhail Gorbachev aptly stated, the Bolsheviks—the godfathers of the communist experiment—carried out a comprehensive "war on religion."[2] Gorbachev lamented that his early predecessors, even after the Russian Civil War ended in the early 1920s, during a time of "peace," had "continued to tear down churches, arrest clergymen, and destroy them. This was no longer understandable or justifiable. Atheism took rather savage forms in our country at that time."[3]

The Soviet Union, reflective of the communist world as a whole, was openly hostile to religion and officially atheist. With (ironically) religious-like devotion, the USSR doggedly took the position that there was no God. Moreover, that atheism translated into a form of vicious anti-religion that included a systematic, often brutal campaign to eliminate belief. This began from the outset of the Soviet state and still continues in various forms in communist countries to this day, from China to North Korea to Cuba.

The roots of this hatred and intolerance of religion lay in the essence of Marxist-Leninist ideology. Karl Marx had dubbed religion the "opiate of the masses," and opined that, "Communism begins where atheism begins."[4] Vladimir Lenin said far worse. Speaking on behalf of the Bolsheviks in his famous October 2, 1920 speech, Lenin stated matter-of-factly: "We do not believe in God." Lenin insisted that "all worship of a divinity is a necrophilia."[5] He wrote in a November 1913 letter that "any religious idea, any idea of any God at all, any flirtation even with a God is the most inexpressible foulness … the most dangerous foulness, the most shameful 'infection.'" Russia scholar James Thrower of the University of Virginia says that in this letter the type of "infection" Lenin was referring to was venereal disease.[6]

"There can be nothing more abominable than religion," wrote Lenin in a letter to Maxim Gorky in January 1913.[7] On December 25, 1919, Christmas Day in the West, Comrade Lenin issued the following order, in his own handwriting: "To put up with 'Nikola' [the religious holiday] would be stupid—the entire Cheka must be on the alert to see to it that those who do not show up for work because of 'Nikola' are shot."[8] Under Lenin, this was not an isolated occurrence.

With Leon Trotsky as his trusty comrade, Lenin became involved in the creation of groups with names like the Society of the Godless, also known as the League of the Militant Godless, which was responsible for the dissemination of anti-religious propaganda in the USSR.[9] Not surprisingly, this institutionalized bigotry continued to thrive under Lenin's disciples, most notably Stalin, and even under more benign leaders like Nikita Khrushchev.

Instilling this atheism was a central goal of communist education, from primary school to the university and even to the factory. Atheism was taught in school. Courses on atheism were mandatory in the Soviet Union. Workers at factories were assembled into meeting rooms where atheist professors from the local university were brought in to deliver lectures on the "stupidity" of "cults" and belief in God.

This atheism was endemic to the communist revolution. Even those communists unable to secure political power—and thus lacking the ability to persecute believers—still did their best to persecute the teachings of organized religion and ridicule the idea of the existence of God. In fact, even in America, it was no surprise to stroll by a city newsstand and catch bold front-page headlines like this in the *Daily Worker*, the communist organ published by CPUSA: "THERE IS NO GOD."[10] Communists were proud of their atheism, and often quite militant about it—and never shy about it.

What I've offered thus far is a kind of snapshot tutorial on the communist war on faith, which traversed national boundaries, ethnicities, and people of every kind throughout the world since 1917. The communists were remarkably consistent in their vicious bigotry toward religion. Alas, I could likewise expound upon added evils wrought by communist hatred, such as the infinitely more painful figures on the unprecedented number of body bags generated by the ideology—easily exceeding 100 million from 1917 to 1979. We now know that even the most authoritative sources, such as the seminal Harvard University Press work, *The Black of Book of Communism*, were conservative when estimating *only* 100 million deaths at the hands of communist governments. The latest research, for instance, claims that Mao Zedong alone was responsible for the deaths of at least 60-70 million in China, and Joseph Stalin alone may well have killed 60 million in the USSR[11]—those are just two communist countries that managed to far surpass the entire combined death toll of World War I and II, the two worst wars in the history of humanity.

Oddly enough, however, this grisly history of Red terror—so recent to the human experience that billions of its persecuted victims remain alive to witness to the atrocity—is too often neglected in the modern classroom at the typical American university. That may seem difficult to believe, but it is true, to the great frustration of those aware of the slight and the slaughter.

I know this very well, and personally, not only as a recent former student myself (I was in graduate school in the 1990s), but as a professor who speaks at colleges around the country. Of all the lectures that I do on college campuses, none seem to awaken the audience as much as my discourse on the savagery of communism. In these lectures, which are usually connected to my study of certain Cold War figures, I do a 10-15 minute backgrounder on the crimes of communists—from their militant attacks on private property, on members of all religious faiths, and on basic civil liberties, to the one product they produced better than any other: bloodied, emaciated, rotting corpses.

As I review the casualties, the students in the audience—born around or after the fall of the Berlin Wall—are amazed at what they are hearing. They seem especially struck that I always ground every fact and figure in reliable research and authorities—books published by the top university presses, quotes from the likes of Mikhail Gorbachev and Vaclav Havel and Alexander Yakovlev, anti-Soviet appraisals from Cold War Democrats like Harry Truman and John F. Kennedy and early liberals like Woodrow Wilson, anti-communist assessments by leftist intellectuals and Cold War scholars like Allen Weinstein, Sam Tanenhaus, Arthur M. Schlesinger, Jr., George F. Kennan, and John Lewis Gaddis. I rarely use conservative sources because I do not want the professors of these students to be able to later poke holes in my presentation to try to undermine the overall thesis.

And speaking of those professors, that gets to the central point of this article: As the young people in the audience are engaged, hands in the air with question after question—obviously hearing all of these things for the first time in their lives (as they are eager to inform me after my talk)—the professors often stare at me with contempt. In one case, a British professor, who could not stop sighing, squirming, and rolling her eyes as I quoted the most heinous assessments of religion by Marx and Lenin—the quotes cited earlier in this article—got up and stormed out of the room.

These professors glare at me as if the ghost of Joe McCarthy has flown into the room and leapt inside of my body. In fact, that is the essence of their criticism: the anti-communism they are witnessing appalls them. It helps explain how, and why, this greatest of human-rights atrocities can be dismissed by so much of the professoriate, which I shall begin to unpack in the next section of this article.

Trends, Fads, and Anti-Anti-Communism

Academia has been beset by many trends, fads, sentiments, and at times outright silly ideas. In more recent years, beginning with the emergence of political correctness on college campuses in the 1980s,[12] academia has offered a sacred-like status to a unique trinity of ethnic, gender, and sexuality diversity. "Diversity" itself has become a kind of idol at the modern university, especially secular colleges.

Of course, that diversity is, ironically, not fully diverse at all; it is very narrowly defined, restricted to ethnicity, gender, and sexual orientation, and is most assuredly not extended to where diversity should matter most at a university: intellectual diversity. Regrettably, diversity of thought, of ideas, and even of religious belief, is not the dominant spirit of the ideologically homogenous modern college. The forces of multiculturalism and "tolerance" can be downright intolerant of beliefs they do not embrace. Really, the phrase "diversity" is a fraud, conveying something else that violates the very meaning of the word.

It is crucial to pause here to note that the disciples of diversity, as well as its bishops, approach the altar from the political left. The diversity movement is a left-of-center movement.

Conservatives are not only not part of the movement—nor welcomed, given their ideology—but their conservatism is considered antithetical to the faith.

This overall leftward tilt of the academy is not disputed by anyone. Survey after survey have shown that upwards of 80-90% of college professors identify themselves as politically liberal,[13] proportions considerably out of sync with the American public, where conservatives outnumber liberals by quite sizable margins, and where Republicans and Democrats are nearly equal among registered voters.[14] This academic bias has made itself obvious, even allowing for those commendable professors who manage to present both sides of an issue. Indeed, liberal professors tend to dispute concerns about the lack of ideological balance by claiming that the imbalance does not matter, since they are professionals capable of being fair in the classroom.[15] The "doesn't-matter" tack is a safer course, far more anecdotal and difficult to prove, especially compared to the easy-to-demonstrate fact (quantifiable via surveys) that most professors are liberal.

Yet, not surprisingly, this staunch left-wing bias influences the way numerous subjects are taught. Among them, one of the longest standing biases in modern academia, stretching all the way back to the 1940s, concerns the subject of communism, and particularly communism in America. Despite the claims of many on the political right, the bias here is not a matter of a huge number of, say, history or sociology or political science professors being Marxists. Many such professors exist, but they are a minority; while colleges lean decidedly left, they do not lean quite *that* far to the left.

Of course, some of the most popular history books ignoring the horrors of communism are written by Marxists, Marxist sympathizers, or general radicals—Eric Hobsbawm, Howard Zinn, Noam Chomsky.[16] Yet, in the vast majority of cases, the bias in the classroom comes not from the pro-communist sympathies of true believers and fellow travelers but from the hearty anti-anti-communist tendencies of non-communist liberals.

The bias regarding communism that exists in modern academia is not one so much of pro-communism—though, as shown below, there are undeniable sympathies—but a very strong dislike, bordering on disgust in many cases, for *anti-communism*. What prevails in modern academia is more a matter of anti-anti-communism than anything else; in other words, these professors are not so much in favor of the communists, but strongly *against* anti-communists.[17] It is not so much that these professors approve of communism as much as they disapprove of—actually, utterly despise—anti-communism. To repeat: they are *anti*-anti-communist more so than pro-communist.

This is also because they reflexively recoil at the right. As James Burnham, the great convert to anti-communism, famously remarked, for the left, "the preferred enemy is always to the right"—never to the left.[18]

So, I implore conservatives to understand this, so as to avoid broad-brushing, losing credibility, and attacking with the same lack of charity and nastiness by which the left frequently engages. Sure, a lot of professors are Marxists, and many more share the utopian goals of Marxism, but the vast majority are simply leftists.

Being on the left often entails some confusing standards, one of which is this bizarre revulsion toward anti-communists. These leftists—to their credit—despise fascism, and will preach anti-fascism until they are blue in the face. They are as appalled by fascism as conservatives are by communism. But while conservatives detest *both* communism and fascism, liberals only detest one of the two.[19]

Why does this matter? Is this a mere academic observation? Not at all.

On a smaller scale, it provides an important political and almost psychological explanation for why these professors think the way they do on this subject. In so doing, it clarifies something that has long baffled both moderates and conservatives alike. It also, thereby, ought to help diffuse conservatives' anger toward these professors, who are often derided, unfairly, as "a bunch of commies," which they are not. At the same time, these professors often defend the commies, while not defending the anti-communists, whom they view with disdain. They are so hostile to the anti-communists that they often refuse to engage in any discussion that might appear to strike a kinship with the beliefs of anti-communists; the end result is an unbalanced presentation that appears more pro-communist.

On a larger scale, this question matters for an important reason pertaining to American higher education, and especially what is being taught in our colleges: The fact is that there was no greater, longer-running conflict in the last 100 years than the grand ideological struggle between Western democratic capitalism and Soviet-based totalitarian communism. This was the dominant battle of the 20th century, fully infusing American and world politics for generations. Even then, it was much more than that, since it involved the slaughter of countless lives.

Consequently, as the carnage alone demonstrates, this subject matters. If professors are to be teachers—teachers of fact, teachers of history, teachers of factual history—here is one issue they need to get right. Quite the contrary, as attested by anyone who has attended these colleges and read the texts, modern academia does a miserable job in underscoring the dark side of communism, a horrible failure that is not at all the case when documenting the crimes of the other vicious "ism" of the last century: Nazi fascism.

Pipes and Brovkin

An especially instructive example of all this can be told through the eyes of two Harvard professors of Russian history: Richard Pipes and Vladimir Brovkin.

Richard Pipes was born in Poland on July 11, 1923. As a 16-year-old Jew at the time of Hitler's invasion, Pipes escaped the country, thanks to a very clever and very wise father, a move that he is convinced saved his life. He credits not only his father for his survival but also providential intervention. That experience, and those that followed, taught Pipes a number of life lessons. In his *Vixi: Memoirs of a Non-Belonger*, he wrote:

> The main effect of the Holocaust on my psyche was to make me delight in every day of life that has been granted to me, for I was saved from certain death. I felt and feel to this day that I have been spared not to waste my life on self-indulgence or self-aggrandizement but to spread a moral message by showing, using examples from history, how evil ideas lead to evil consequences. Since scholars have written enough on the Holocaust, I thought it my mission to demonstrate this truth using the example of communism.

Pipes would do exactly that.

Pipes arrived in the United States in July 1940. He ultimately earned a doctorate in history at Harvard in 1950. He would spend the next 50-plus years at Harvard, where he was professor of Russian history, director of the Russian Research Center, and is now Principal Investigator of the excellent Harvard Project on Cold War Studies. He was always well-received at Harvard. His classes were large and full. In 1996, he retired from the classroom, though his association with Harvard continues as, among other things, Baird Professor of History, Emeritus. Among his most important publications are

Russia Under the Old Regime (1974), *The Russian Revolution* (1990), *Russia Under the Bolshevik Regime* (1994), *The Unknown Lenin: From the Secret Archive* (1996), and *Communism: A History* (2001).

For decades, Pipes has been consistently attacked by liberal colleagues for being too harsh on communism. In 2005, I interviewed Pipes about this phenomenon. He visited Grove City College at the invitation of the Center for Vision & Values to deliver the annual J. Howard Pew Lecture. Here's an excerpt:

> Q: Dr. Pipes, academic historians have done an extremely thorough, commendable job documenting the horrors and crimes of the fascist Nazis but not the communist Bolsheviks. Why is that?
>
> Pipes: This is quite true. And the answer is difficult. One reason is that many of them [academic historians] politically agree, at least in theory, with many of the goals of the communists—equal distribution of wealth and income equality, for example. Certainly this is one reason. In practice, though, they [communist regimes] achieved none of this. In practice, communism was sheer barbarism. Intellectuals love ideas, and they loved many of these ideas—so, they tolerated even many of the negatives of communism. When I pointed out many of these negatives in *The Russian Revolution*, I was accused of being bitter and unduly harsh.
>
> Q: That's an accusation that historians of the Nazis were never charged with….
>
> Pipes: Yes, that's right.

Q: What explains this double standard? This bias within academia? This unwillingness to dwell on the evils of Bolshevism and communism generally? I heard an interview with Robert Conquest [Hoover Institution, Stanford], who said that while the reason is rooted in the leftist bias of academics, it is not the result of pro-communism by these academics but, rather, the result of "anti-anti-communism." In other words, said Conquest, they dislike the anti-communists. In fact, it seems they detest the anti-communists and view them in much lower repute than even the communists. Does anti-anti-communism explain this?

Pipes: Yes, that's quite right. Academics consider anti-communism and anti-communists to be vulgar and simple-minded. There are very few communists [among these academics], but many, many anti-anti-communists. Plus, they say they need to be impartial in dealing with the Bolsheviks, for example, rather than condemning them in their scholarship—which, in actual effect, in practice, can mean being supportive.... They were rightly partial in dealing with Auschwitz, while, in many cases, ignoring the gulag.

Q: When I speak at universities on the subject of Bolshevik crimes and the Soviet war on religion, and I list death tallies and share horrific quotes from Lenin and Stalin, most of the audience is riveted, as if I'm providing completely new information (which, to them, I am), whereas professors in the crowd sometimes glare at me with contemptuous looks....

Pipes: That's not a surprise.

Q: You say that there is more to the question of this Nazi-Bolshevik double standard among academic Sovietologists; that the question is complicated, and there's more to the answer. Could you elaborate?

Pipes: Well, it is a very complicated question.... Again, one reason why intellectuals are so much more obsessed with Nazi crimes than Soviet crimes — even though in terms of human lives lost the Soviets way exceeded the Nazis — is that intellectuals, by the very nature of their professions, grant enormous attention to words and ideas. And they are attracted by socialist ideas.[20] They find that the ideas of communism are praiseworthy and attractive; that, to them, is more important than the practice of communism. Now, Nazi ideals, on the other hand, were pure barbarism; nothing more could be said in favor of them. In the case of the Soviet Union, [intellectuals] could say, "Well, yes, the practice of Soviet communism was perhaps quite bad, but the ideas are wonderful, and if we did not disturb the Soviets and did not fight them or resist them, but, instead, helped them, they might have realized these ideas."

A second reason is that Germany is in the heart of Europe; it is one of the great civilizations of Europe. Therefore, what happens there affects us in the West far more than what happens in outlying areas. Russia is on the periphery of Europe. We see this today, where there are horrible atrocities committed in the Third World and we don't get very upset about it. If what happened in Russia under the communists had happened in a Western European country, everyone would have been upset by it.

Q: What about the Bolsheviks' brutal persecution of religious believers? Haven't historians ignored this as well?

Pipes: Yes. In fact, in *Russia Under the Bolshevik Regime*, I devoted a full chapter to the persecution of the Church. To my knowledge, this was the only history of the Russian revolution to include that focus. In [Edward H.] Carr's history and others, there's virtually nothing on the subject.... Russia was a very religious country. It's quite true that the subject has received little to virtually no attention from scholars.

Q: Your book on the Lenin letters, *The Unknown Lenin*, was so crucially important in exposing the real Lenin, the monstrous Lenin, and what Lenin was all about—

Pipes: —but it got almost no attention.

Q: No attention?

Pipes: No. The book did not sell many copies. That's because it depicted Lenin as he really was. And the whole establishment, [including academic Sovietologists in the West,] wanted to depict Lenin as an idealist who was betrayed by Stalin. So, when you have these letters that show how cruel Lenin really was.... They simply didn't want to talk about it. One reviewer on Amazon actually said that I fabricated the letters! Others said, "Well, you show only the nasty side of Lenin."...

By earning tenure early in his career, and before anti-anti-communism pervaded academia, Pipes managed to survive the condemnation of his colleagues for daring to be so harsh on communism. Unfortunately, a close colleague of Pipes was not able to survive. That colleague is Vladimir Brovkin, who came to Harvard 40 years after Pipes first arrived, and was unable to quickly secure the shield of tenure he would need to fend off the intellectual left.

Like Pipes, Vladimir Brovkin, as a young man, escaped totalitarianism. For Brovkin, however, it was the totalitarianism of the far left—the brand that much of the academic left is loath to condemn. He is a survivor of the communist slave state, with indispensible firsthand knowledge of what Boris Yeltsin called the "horror house" that was the Soviet Union.

A native Russian, Brovkin graduated from Leningrad University in 1973. He came to the United States to earn a master's degree in Russian studies from Georgetown in 1977 before earning a Ph.D. in history at Princeton in 1984. Having successfully escaped the USSR, Brovkin became a U.S. resident, publishing three books on the Soviet Union and joining the faculty at Harvard as an associate professor of history in 1990.

Yet, in short order, by the late 1990s, Brovkin was being railroaded by fellow Sovietologists for being too anti-Soviet. A series of works on communism that he planned to write for Yale University Press was rejected because of what his critics called the "excessively 'anti-Bolshevik' tone" of his work. The alleged problem was evident in the heart of Brovkin's proposal for the series, especially his desire to focus on the gulag, where he endeavored to explain "how and why a monstrous system of mass terror came into being." Such an approach, claimed one of the reviewers who rejected Brovkin's proposal, would "threaten the scholarly reputation of the entire project." Another reviewer complained that Brovkin had failed to

Anti-Anti-Communism and the Academy

understand that Soviet prisoners were sent to the gulag "in accordance with the laws of the land."[21]

This criticism would be amusing if not so sad. Imagine, by comparison, a scholar on the Nazi concentration camps being chided for not understanding that Jews were sent to Auschwitz and Bergen-Belsen "in accordance with the laws of the land." Indeed, precisely that thought occurred to Dr. Pipes, who a half-century earlier had Jewish friends and relatives sent to such places, where they died. Remarking on Brovkin's critics, Pipes noted: "I've never seen a respectable historian criticize a German scholar for demonizing Hitler or being too anti-Nazi."[22]

Pipes, who was there at Harvard with Brovkin in the 1990s, agrees that Brovkin got in trouble because he was considered "too passionately anti-communist" and had indeed "demonize[d] the Soviet regime."[23]

Brovkin would face excommunication for his sin of anti-communism. It was for such reasons, he says, that he was denied tenure at Harvard and eventually sent packing, exiled to the academic gulag of anti-communists who dare to criticize the USSR. Says Pipes of the revisionists who have blacklisted Brovkin: "they make it very hard for anyone who holds a different point of view to get a job. [Brovkin] is a very good example."[24]

Jacob Heilbrunn, the senior editor at *The New Republic*—the always honest, always interesting bible of the left—who highlighted Brovkin's troubles in the 1990s, was even harsher to the revisionists: "The Soviet studies field has been captured by revisionists who dismiss as Cold War humbug the notion that the Soviet Union was a totalitarian country.... These American revisionists are spouting the same propaganda the Soviet government dispensed from the 1920s onward."[25]

Brovkin is today a teacher in a high school in Florida, having not attained the "proper" worldview of the professoriate. Brovkin has been blacklisted for his anti-communism.

"Insane" Solzhenitsyn

It will astound many to read this, but another Russian often dismissed around the faculty club was no less than the face of the gulag itself: Alexander Solzhenitsyn, the greatest of dissidents. One example was shared with me by Mark Hendrickson, economics professor of Grove City College, immediately after the recent August 2008 death of the esteemed anti-communist, who died at the age of 89.

It is impossible to adequately capture here what Solzhenitsyn meant, lived, and how he went about translating it to the West in a special way, most notably through his majestic, *The Gulag Archipelago*, and *One Day in the Life of Ivan Denisovich*, both shocking, autobiographical, Nobel winning, firsthand accounts of the Soviet forced-labor-camp system. These books hit the world in the 1970s, when much of the truth about the Soviet system had not been known, and certainly never so concisely and gruelingly telegraphed as in the pages of Solzhenitsyn. His groundbreaking work unearthed gem after gem to an outside world not yet fully acquainted with the awful Soviet state.

Solzhenitsyn's salvos in the 1970s, thanks to the unfiltered voice of a free American press, exploded like cannon fire at the Iron Curtain. The Soviets recoiled each time Solzhenitsyn's words were broadcast in the West, enraged that he had survived the gulag to blow the whistle and tell the truth to a world that needed to hear it—including to American college students who were often being indoctrinated into believing that the systems of the United States and USSR were morally equivalent. That brings me to Mark Hendrickson's experience.

Hendrickson recalls being handed *One Day in the Life of Ivan Denisovich* in January 1974 as a young student at Oxford, given the book as his first assignment by the great Miltonian scholar Archie Burnett. Prior to that, not more than two years earlier, Hendrickson had considered himself a socialist, maybe even a communist. The book was a thunderbolt. "After reading this book," said Hendrickson, "I forever closed the door on my youthful flirtation with Big Government."[26]

On the other hand, some of those who badly needed to hear the message of Solzhenitsyn did not want to hear it, including some in the United States, namely in the academy. As Hendrickson recalled, the message "didn't stop many liberals in the West from remaining active apologists for the Soviet communists." Quite the contrary, Solzhenitsyn had made them angry, angry not at Soviet communism but at Solzhenitsyn—at the *anti-communism* on display by the dissident. Hendrickson recalls: "One liberal professor stridently told me that Solzhenitsyn belonged in an insane asylum."

This was more than a distasteful, ridiculous remark by the professor. It was actually a literal Soviet talking point. As Hendrickson notes, this was "a telling remark, since the Soviets themselves used insane asylums as a preferred place of imprisonment for dissident intellectuals."

That is absolutely correct. One who suffered such humiliating treatment was Vladimir Bukovsky, who spent 12 years in the Soviet gulag system, where he was shifted between work camps, prisons, and lunatic asylums, and ultimately treated as a madman for not thoroughly enjoying the utopian paradise.[27] Bukovsky was likely in a nuthouse at the very moment that the liberal American professor suggested to Hendrickson that Solzhenitsyn be sent to one as well.

Indeed, the U.S. Congress, at this same time, was researching this issue anew. In the summer of 1976, the U.S. House subcommittee on international political and military affairs heard testimony on Soviet torture of religious believers. Witnesses spoke of the routine mental abuse pursued in state experimental camps and psychiatric clinics, where Christians in particular were abused. As one dissident put it, Christians were "treated for their faith," often by heavy drug sedation, as well as the newer tactic that dissidents termed "physical annihilation."[28]

It was so bad in the Soviet Union that for the first time in U.S. history, the Congress—Democrats and Republicans alike—went on record approving a resolution condemning Soviet persecution of Christians specifically and the insane-asylum treatment generally. It passed 381 to 2 in the House in October 1976.[29] And yet, this was nothing compared to the 1920s and 1930s and what Solzhenitsyn himself had witnessed.

The professor who made that point, notes Hendrickson, was not a communist, but a liberal anti-anti-communist. He was most assuredly unwittingly toeing the Moscow line. The professor was, plainly, a dupe, unknowingly doing the truly dirty work of Solzhenitsyn's torturers. As for the great dissident, it was no surprise to be told he was crazy by his Soviet tormentors inside the Gulag Archipelago, but it would have floored him to hear the charge from an American professor with a PhD.

Trickle-Down Civics

There are numerous such examples of this anti-anti-communism that could be cited in this article. One more focus, however, is crucial. Notably, this final case floats between anti-anti-communism and pro-communism, and—sadly—directly into our public schools.

This ideological mindset within the academy has had a terrible trickle-down effect on the teaching of these subjects in high schools. That should not be a surprise, given that the history/civics texts used in high schools are written by these same professors. I know this in an informed, systematic way, given that I was hired to conduct a comprehensive, two-year study on "World History" and "Civics" texts used in high schools. The June 2002 study, which is available on the Internet, looked at roughly 20 texts used in public schools in the state of Wisconsin, which are generally the same texts used in public schools throughout the United States, given that there is little variation from state to state.[30]

The treatment of communism in these texts is both depressing and an outrage. The greatest abuse is the sins of omission: what is not covered. I could not find a single text that listed figures on the total number of deaths by communist governments, even though data was provided in other categories, such as war-time deaths—and even though new, widely publicized data had just been made available in seminal, respected post-Cold War works like *The Black Book of Communism*.

These texts' failure to highlight the historical scourge of communism was not repeated for historical events like the Inquisition, the Crusades, slavery, the internment of Japanese Americans—which, incidentally, never mentioned Franklin Delano Roosevelt's role—or other tragic episodes that featured infinitely lower casualties. "Right-wing" dictators like Cuba's Batista and Chile's Pinochet were treated far more harshly than Fidel Castro, who generated far more victims and was still in power.

Likewise, the treatment of Red China was extraordinarily weak, including no condemnations of modern human-rights crimes like the one-child policy. To the contrary, the texts offered outright rosy descriptions of life in the contemporary Chinese classroom and of "youth groups" like the Young Pioneers. One text, titled, *Global Insights*, served up this glossy sidebar on Chinese "Young People:"

> Although Chinese students work hard at their studies, they still find time to participate in activities outside of school. Many young people are involved in youth organizations. The Young Pioneers is a children's organization to which about 50 percent of China's youngsters belong. Its purpose is to train children to be good citizens. The Communist Youth League, on the other hand, is an honor organization for high school students. To become a member, a student

must be at least 15 years of age and have an excellent academic and political record.[31]

This brief, cheery section, which includes no critical examination or explanation — I've quoted the section in its entirety, with nothing omitted — is followed up by a touching profile of a Chinese Olympic gymnast. It literally reads like official agitprop from the Chinese Central Committee.

The same text makes the indefensible claim that Mao's Great Leap Forward — which, it neglects to note, created the largest mass starvation in the history of the world, with roughly 60 million deaths in about four years — enabled China to "make significant economic gains under communist rule. By the mid-1960s, it was ranked among the ten leading industrial nations in the world."

Most offensive in these high-school texts was the downright bizarre claim — made by more than one text — that communism, whether in the USSR or Mao's People's Republic of China, was a historic, glorious triumph for women. In regard to the first decade of the Bolshevik revolution, one text explained: "legally speaking, Russian women were better off than women anywhere in the world."[32]

That claim, obviously, is utterly absurd. How could it be remotely possible? What evidence might be somehow summoned by the professors who wrote the text? The authors provide an explanation in the next sentence: Russian girls as early as 1920 had access to abortion.

None of this is a surprise, given that these texts are written by modern professors. You reap what you sow.

And, naturally, this trickles down to the classroom. Teachers are always asked to teach subjects that they do not know — or, at the least, subjects in which they are lacking expertise. In those frequent cases, as any high-school teacher will admit, the teacher refers students to the text: "For the exam, read pages

120 to 130 on Castro's Cuba." That is an inevitable, albeit gloomy, prospect.

As far as the effect on individual teachers in the classroom, I could share innumerable personal examples from my own experience and from reports by former students who have entered the classroom as teachers.

One former student, John, Grove City College class of 2000, told me about his first assignment as a teaching assistant in a high-school history class about 30 miles from Grove City, Pennsylvania. John, who had been a double major at Grove City, both education and history, offered to cover some of the lectures on the Soviet Union in the 1930s. His supervising teacher agreed. So, John methodically covered the famine in the Ukraine, Stalin's purges and Red Terror, the Hitler-Stalin Pact, and gave carefully sourced figures on the millions of Stalin's victims. It is flatly impossible to give anything but a negative account of Stalin in the 1930s; a biased presentation would be a lecture that was *not* negative. To live in the USSR in the 1930s was to live one of the worst nightmares in human history.

John was pleased at how the students were electrified, many hands in the air, many questions—clearly learning all of these hideous things for the first time in their lives. Yet, he also noticed the dirty looks from his supervisor stationed at the back of the room. At the end of John's presentation, the teacher testily reprimanded him: "Look, John, I want you to ease up on the Red-baiting and commie-bashing. Besides, these students are going to get a decidedly different view on communism from me." She promised to teach "a softer side of communism."

Imagine this situation in reverse and applied to, say, Nazism. The teacher would be written up in the local newspaper and probably fired.

Another student of mine, Sean, Grove City College class of 2001, told me of the elite Christian private school he attended in the Cleveland area, where the newly hired teacher, fresh out of college from a major university in Pennsylvania, told the students that he was a "Christian communist," and that anyone who is a Christian should be a communist. "Communism is misunderstood," was the teacher's refrain.

That was also the argument pushed by a teacher in the Allegheny County school district, which was relayed to me by a freshman student in a 1996 course I taught at Robert Morris University. This young woman was angry. She said the teacher had "convinced" the entire class that Marxism was a "wonderful" but "misunderstood" system that simply had not been tried correctly. "He absolutely brainwashed us," she told me.

These are merely three anecdotal examples. Honestly, I have never had an occasion where some young person has not paused to tell me stories like this after I have completed a lecture on the atrocities of communism. The students are often quite bitter, as if they have been misled, misinformed, and betrayed.

* * *

The leftist intelligentsia that dominates higher education, and which writes the history/civics texts used in high schools, and which trains the teachers who teach in high schools, is not in the slightest bit notably anti-communist. Generally, these non-communist liberals do not teach the correct, crucial lessons of communism.

What is more, aside from failing to instruct their students in the crass facts about communism's unprecedented destruction—its purges, mass famines, show trials, killing fields, concentration camps—these educators are negligent in failing to teach the essential, non-emotional, but crucial Econ 101 basics that contrast capitalism and communism and, thus, that get at the heart of how and why command economies simply do not work. Each semester in my Comparative Politics course at Grove City College, it takes no more than 30 minutes to matter-of-factly lay out the rudimentary differences: Whereas capitalist systems are based on the market forces of supply and demand, which dictate prices and production levels and targets, communist systems are based on central planning, by which a government bureau attempts to manage such things. The former system is based on private ownership; the latter on public ownership. The former thrives on small government and taxes; the latter on large government and taxes, typically progressive income-tax rates and estate taxes—both advocated explicitly by Marx—and much more.

This material is not rocket science. It is easy to teach, if the professor desires. The problem is that it is too often willfully neglected and not being taught. Consequently, Americans today do not know why communism is such a devastating ideology, at both the level of plain economic theory and in actual historical practice. It is a remarkably hateful system, based on targeted annihilation of entire classes and groups of people, which its practitioners have candidly conceded since 1917.[33] (Nazism sought genocide based on ethnicity; communism sought genocide based on class.)

Most Americans generally know that the USSR was a bad place and that it was good that the Berlin Wall fell; they lived through that. But they know little beyond that, especially young Americans in college today, born around or after the time the wall fell. The current generation of college students was not inspired by JFK's or Ronald Reagan's speeches near the Berlin Wall, by Pope John Paul II's pilgrimage to Poland in 1979, by Margaret Thatcher or Mikhail Gorbachev, by Vaclav Havel or Lech Walesa, by the Solidarity or Charter 77 movements, by the Hungarian uprising of 1956 or the Prague Spring of 1968. No, today's freshmen, sophomores, juniors, and seniors, who voted for the first time on November 4, 2008, were born after these historic events. They have received their education on communism from their professors, which means they have received either little or no education at all on the unparalleled slaughter formally known as Marxism-Leninism, or, to the contrary, they have heard only dark, dire lectures about the malevolence of anti-communism—of McCarthyism. They have been carefully trained to view Joe McCarthy as more insidious than Joe Stalin.

All of this makes Americans not only ignorant of communism but prone to support far-left economic policies or to elect people who have been mentored by communists, have links to communists, or subscribe to forms of socialism. An American politician could literally run for office with a slogan of "From each according to his abilities, to each according to his needs," and a shockingly large segment of the public would have no idea what was being espoused.[34] The nation is now extremely vulnerable to the very ideas of collectivism and redistribution that it vanquished in the Cold War.

Moreover, because of the leftist establishment's indoctrination of anti-anti-communism, the left creates bad guys out of the anti-communists who are legitimately blowing the whistle on policies or policy-makers pushing concepts rooted in or resembling Marxist thinking. When the 1960s leftists started saturating higher education—as well as the media—they really knew what they were doing. This was a coup for them and their worldview, with ripple effects we can scarcely imagine.

The Santayana aphorism is correct: those who do not remember the past are condemned to repeat it. For decades now, we have not taught the next generation what it needs to know from its immediate past. It will come back to bite us, if it has not already. We won the Cold War but are in danger of losing the ideological debate at home. We lost not on the battlefield but in the classroom. It has been a remarkable victory for the anti-anti-communists of the academy.

¹ Pipes said this in an interview that I did with him during a visit to Grove City College on September 27, 2005, where he gave the annual Pew Lecture. That interview will be further referenced throughout this article.

² Mikhail Gorbachev, *Memoirs* (NY: Doubleday, 1996), p. 328.

³ Mikhail Gorbachev, *On My Country and the World*, (NY: Columbia University Press, 2000), pp. 20-1.

⁴ The "opiate of the masses" remark is well-known. The source for the quote, "communism begins where atheism begins," is Fulton J. Sheen, *Communism and the Conscience of the West* (Indianapolis and NY: Bobbs-Merrill, 1948). Sheen, who spoke and read several languages, translated the quote into English from an un-translated Marx work.

⁵ Lenin wrote this in a November 13 or 14, 1913 letter to Maxim Gorky. See: James Thrower, *God's Commissar: Marxism-Leninism as the Civil Religion of Soviet Society* (Lewiston, NY: Edwin Mellen Press, 1992), p. 39.

⁶ Quoted in Thrower, *God's Commissar*, p. 39. Another translation of this quote comes from Robert Conquest, in his "The Historical Failings of CNN," in Arnold Beichman, ed., *CNN's Cold War Documentary* (Stanford, CA: Hoover Institution Press, 2000), p. 57.

⁷ See: J. M. Bochenski, "Marxism-Leninism and Religion," in B. R. Bociurkiw et al, eds., *Religion and Atheism in the USSR and Eastern Europe* (London: MacMillan, 1975), p. 11.

⁸ This item was published in a 2002 book by Yale University Press. See: Alexander N. Yakovlev, *A Century of Violence in Soviet Russia* (New Haven and London: Yale University Press, 2002), p. 157.

⁹ See: Daniel Peris, *Storming the Heavens: The Soviet League of the Militant Godless* (Ithaca, NY: Cornell University Press, 1998).

¹⁰ See: Bertram D. Wolfe, *A Life in Two Centuries* (Stein and Day, 1981), pp. 403-4.

¹¹ Alexander Yakovlev, the reformer and close Gorbachev adviser, who in the 1990s was tasked with trying to tally Stalin's victims, reports the 60-million figure in his seminal work published by Yale University Press. See: Yakovlev, *A Century of Violence in Soviet Russia.*

¹² The seminal early work on this subject was Dinesh D'Souza's ground-breaking 1991 book and excerpted article, "Illiberal Education," which ran as the cover feature in *The Atlantic Monthly.*

¹³ These surveys are easy to track down. I cited several of them in Paul Kengor, "Reagan Among the Professors," *Policy Review*, December 1999 / January 2000. Among data I cited was the fact that Stanford's department of history had 22 Democrats but just two Republicans; Dartmouth had 10 Democrats and zero Republicans; Cornell had 29 Democrats and not a single Republican. Reflecting the sort of political diversity seen in Castro's

Cuba and the Ayatollah's theocracy, the University of Colorado-Boulder registers stupefying single-party numbers: In the departments of history, English, and philosophy there were 68 Democrats but no Republicans, according to a survey in the late 1990s. Of the 190 professors surveyed in the university's social sciences and humanities department, 184 are Democrats and six are Republicans. A nation-wide poll from the early 1990s found 88% of "public affairs" faculty identifying themselves as liberal, 12% claiming to be "middle of the road" and, remarkably, 0% opting for the conservative label.

[14] Self-identified conservatives and registered Republicans have declined during the unpopular presidency of Republican George W. Bush. Still, the number of registered Republicans is very similar to the number of Democrats, and self-identified conservatives usually rank around 40% of the public, compared to liberals who fall somewhere in mid- to upper-20% range.

[15] For yet another interesting twist on this defense, see: Patricia Cohen, "Professors' Liberalism Contagious? Maybe Not," *The New York Times*, November 3, 2008.

[16] Among these, see Eric Hobsbawm, *The Age of Extremes* (NY: Vintage, 1994).

[17] I first heard this observation on "anti-anti-communism" from Robert Conquest during a July 1994 interview of Conquest by William F. Buckley Jr. on Buckley's PBS's series, "Firing Line."

[18] Burnham said this in his classic, *Suicide of the West*, first published in 1964.

[19] For instance, the flagship conservative publication *Human Events* recently created a list of top 10 worst books ever written, which included, as the top two, Marx's *Communist Manifesto* (#1), followed by Hitler's *Mein Kampf* (#2). That ranking is easily defended solely on numbers: Hitler killed at least 10 million; communism killed at least 100 million. Either way, *Human Events*, a conservative newspaper, deserves to be commended for putting both communism and fascism in its top two. Yet, conversely, any liberal version of such a list would not even place the *Communist Manifesto* in the top 10. One could be almost certain that liberals who read the *Human Events* list snickered at its alleged Neanderthal anti-communism.

[20] Liberals agree with communists on many key sympathies: workers' rights, the spreading and redistribution of wealth, a narrow income gap, a wide array of "free" government services, a favoring of the public sector over the private sector, class-based demagoguery toward the wealthy, progressively high tax rates, an expansive central government, a cynicism about business and capitalism, to name a few. The differences are typically matters of degree rather than principle.

21 Robert Stacy McCain, "'Revisionists close the book on Soviet historian," *The Washington Times*, October 19-25, 1998 (National Weekly Edition), p. 14.

22 Ibid.

23 Ibid.

24 Ibid.

25 Ibid.

26 Mark W. Hendrickson, "Thank you, Alexander Solzhenitsyn," Townhall.com, August 8, 2008.

27 This information is based on an interview I did with Vladimir Bukovsky on March 5, 2003.

28 Janis Johnson, "Movement Grows in Congress for Soviet Christian Support," *Washington Post*, July 31, 1976, p. A3. Also see: "Seven Soviet Christians Appeal to World for Aid," *Religious News Services* (published in the *Washington Post*), August 13, 1980, p. C6.

29 Janis Johnson, "Congress Decries Soviet Christian Persecution," *Washington Post*, October 8, 1976, p. B18; and Johnson, "Movement Grows," p. A3.

30 See: Paul Kengor, *Evaluating World History Texts in Wisconsin Public High Schools*, Wisconsin Policy Research Institute, June 2002, Volume 15, No. 4. The website for the report is www.wpri.org.

31 Ibid, p. 21.

32 Ibid, pp. 13-15.

33 "We are exterminating the bourgeoisie as a class," explained a candid M.Y. Latsis, Lenin's ferocious Latvian henchman. See: George Leggett, *The Cheka: Lenin's Political Police* (NY: Oxford University Press, 1981), p. 103.

34 See the shocking results of the economic literacy survey released in November 2008 by the Intercollegiate Studies Institute. Also, one of the top three syndicated talk-show hosts during the 2008 presidential-election season asked supporters of Barack Obama if they agreed with Obama's slogan, "From each according to his abilities, to each according to his needs." The Obama supporters eagerly agreed, not realizing the host was tricking them by quoting Karl Marx. In the 2008 election, I had numerous exchanges with people who said things like, "Even if Obama is a socialist, why would that be a bad thing?" or "So what if he's a socialist, or even if he's a communist. He has a right to believe that in America." The concern, of course, is not whether an American has that right — we have that right — but whether such a person, assuming the person truly believed those things, should be president of the United States of America. The point here is not to assert that Obama is a socialist, but, rather, to emphasize the

critical that point that if he were a socialist, or a Democrat concealing socialist-Marxist beliefs, most Americans would neither recognize the difference nor even care. That is at least in part because of very poor education.

Stalinism Lite

Scott Herring

It is impossible for those outside of literature departments to understand how weird such departments have become. You can see the evidence from without, but only within can you drink deep of our Stalinism Lite. What surprised me, however — what took me years to understand — was that even if I disguised myself as a "liberal," that would not be good enough. The bigger surprise was that the students themselves taught me that lesson, and not because they were angry that I was not leftist enough. I have been lucky, and I can show that there is an audience out there, among the undergrads, that asks, that hungers, for what we have to offer: professors who exhibit simple sanity.

Proving my point will require some background. Unlike most of the authors in this volume, I would not call myself a "conservative," not exactly. My position is a common one for people my age. I am in my late forties, and spent the 1980s as a simon-pure young-intellectual Reagan-hater, one of millions. I can date my conversion to a single minute in time, or maybe five minutes, just after 11:30 p.m., February 27, 1991. An article of faith for the undergraduate Reagan-hater was that the stupid, *stupid* stupidity of the imbecile was most obvious in his moronic confrontation with the invincible Soviet Union. The Soviet Union! We were going to confront the Soviet Union, which had never lost a fight, with our pathetic Army and Navy, bringing to the battle only their stoner personnel and wretched, rubbishy weapons. Every journalist who addressed the issue, every single one, had assured me that US soldiers and sailors were as dense as the President himself, were losers who could not get real jobs, and none of his expensive weapons systems worked. On that point they were relentless: the cruise missiles, the stealthy warplanes, the very rifles and ammo were all worthless.

The implosion of Warsaw-Pact communism in 1989 had shaken my faith, but the literal moment of truth came that night, February 27, 1991, when I turned on the ABC News program *Nightline*, my only source of information at that hour, in that pre-Internet era. The Persian Gulf War had entered its cataclysmic finale. That worthless Army of ours was fighting an Iraq equipped almost entirely with communist weapons. Rumors of colossal tank battles had filtered out of the desert all day. I was genuinely frightened when I turned on the TV, picturing all those thousands of innocent American soldiers, dead and not even recoverable in their still-burning vehicles.

And *Nightline* reported—to its embarrassment, I think—that it was the communist equipment that was burning. The war was all but over. Our supposedly worthless Army had triumphed so completely that *Nightline* could not for the moment even report any U.S. casualties, just Iraqis, thousands and thousands of Iraqis, whose only hope was surrender.

I understood in an instant that I had been systematically lied to for an entire decade. Everything I thought I knew about military affairs was wrong, every single thing. From that moment, I adopted a wait-and-see pragmatism. I assumed that my knowledge of politics was so warped by agenda-driven journalism that I could not form an intelligible opinion on anything, until events told me what was really going on.

Hit the fast-forward button on the 1980s VCR. I spent much of the 1990s in Yellowstone National Park, working for one of the smaller concessionaires and getting deeply addicted to the place. I at last came to understand that I could not make a career out of looking at the scenery (the standard ranger joke is that they get paid in sunsets). I got an M.A. at my undergrad Cal State school, and leveraged my way up several prestige-rungs to the University of California, Davis, where I finished a Ph.D. in English dated September 14, 2001. The economy had already been in recession when the other events of that month made it clear that full-time tenure-track jobs teaching literature would go only to a lucky few.

Fortune favors the prepared, and I had prepared with what now strikes me as callous cynicism. I had written my dissertation about literature and the national parks. Yellowstone had prepared me as thoroughly for that topic as possible, and the University of Virginia Press liked it enough to publish it right away. UC Davis gave me a two-year fellowship, and in its last year my department gave me the course that was clearly intended to be my rehearsal for the job search: Literature of the Wilderness.

Hold on: let me catch you before you reel backwards from the hippie aroma (body odor, patchouli oil, and dope) wafting off the name of that course. It need not have been a travesty. Taking just the nineteenth century, and just the United States, we can think of plenty of authors who will fit into the syllabus, and have earned our respect: Henry David Thoreau, Nathaniel Hawthorne, Mark Twain, John Muir, Willa Cather, Theodore Roosevelt…the list could go on.

You can see the problem for the job seeker. Every person on that list except Cather has long since been convicted, in the court of professorial opinion, of the three mortal sins, Racism, Sexism, and Homophobia. We do not need to rehearse the heresy trials here. I knew that I needed some artificial Diversity on the syllabus, and I needed it right away.

Cather enabled me to check the "feminist" and "queer" boxes, but I otherwise ran into a wall. I knew from living in an actual wilderness that it has little appeal to blacks and Latinos, and even to the Sioux, Cheyenne, Crow, and other tribes that lived right next-door. The National Park Service is aware, too, and it mortifies them to admit, but places like Yellowstone are mainly of interest to whites and Asians. The reason is obvious, although I seem to be the only person to have noticed. If an author is black, or from Mexico or Central America, or an Indian reservation, the city represents a place of opportunity, at least. The countryside is the place where that person's grandparents, or parents, or maybe the author himself suffered under brutal, grinding poverty. The outdoors have no happy associations, and the author is no more likely to describe them than I am likely to detail the contents of my garbage.

A fellow graduate student who was a Maoist came to my aid. She was literally a Maoist, even displaying a picture of the Chairman on her desk, which caused the undergrads to occasionally remark that they would not have guessed that she had a Chinese grandparent. What the Chinese students thought, they kept a secret. She told me to use Luther Standing Bear, a Sioux born in the 1860s and raised in the traditional Sioux ways. I was so desperate that I put him on the syllabus without reading the book.

But I had the sense not to force the students to pay for what amounted to a pedagogical gamble. Instead, I photocopied chunks of the book, *Land of the Spotted Eagle*, and handed them out for free.

And was glad I had done so when I finally read the passages that I had chosen merely because they used the word "nature" regularly. My face went red with deep embarrassment. The book is not only clumsy. It is the single most wildly racist document I have ever seen. Joseph Goebbels himself would never have allowed his Reich Ministry of Public Enlightenment and Propaganda to release anything quite so silly. The Sioux, according to Mr. Bear, were the only perfect people ever to exist, whites the only perfectly evil people. That was the overt theme of every sentence. I kept my calm. *The students are English majors*, I thought. *They'll swallow it.*

The day came, and I had been teaching long enough to recognize a classroom in which intellectual mutiny had already broken forth. Every eyebrow was raised. I tried feebly to talk the book up, but almost the first question went to the heart of the matter. The student—she was the one with all the tattoos, I remember, tattoos like a Papuan headhunter—the student pointed to a passage in which Standing Bear claimed, in all seriousness, that no Sioux ever got sick or hurt before the white people came. "Is he serious?"

"I...um...."

The student with the Abbie Hoffman hair pointed to another bit, one in which Standing Bear claimed what we would call psychic powers for the Sioux, before those powers were taken away by the whites. "Does he really mean this?"

"Maybe...it's...well, you all know what a metaphor is."

Not buying it. The woman who was about my age, and had been enthusiastically on my side from the start, pointed to the lines in which the Sioux were never hungry before the whites took all the food away. She merely read them and looked up with that pointed eyebrow.

Students can smell a lie. They also liked me, and they will accept a half-truth if it defuses embarrassment. "Actually, I put this on the syllabus because I hoped you would spot this stuff. It's what every New Age-type mystic says about people like the Sioux. Why do people enjoy believing these things?" We proceeded to "deconstruct" the photocopied wisdom of Luther Standing Bear, and during the next class session turned with pleasure and relief to John Muir.

The job search was already underway. I applied to over a hundred positions, had seven interviews, and never came close to getting a job, despite the convincing imitation of leftist conformity I produced. I was not discriminated against: eight or ten UC Davis English Ph.D.s went on the market that year, and none of us succeeded, no matter how Diverse. The economy had turned so sour that only an Ivy League Ph.D. stood any chance at even the worst position.

My luck, however, then turned as good as it had been awful. My university moved the writing instructors out of English and into a new department, the University Writing Program. I also got married, and my wife is a physician. In a humanities department, that made me an expert on medicine, so I started teaching advanced writing to the pre-meds and pre-dentals. It became a specialty, and I later figured out how to teach students of the other hard sciences as well. And those students continued to teach me.

I have not had to face the persecution that our host, Mary Grabar, has (of course, neither have I sought controversy much). I also have the advantage of working at the single UC that is dominated, more than any other, by the most pragmatic — and honorable — pursuits, milk production, crop genomics, veterinary medicine, and so on. The students are mostly apolitical. It is a measure of the malign effect a few of the more wild-eyed professors can have that, at that rally Mary describes in the introduction, they were able to whip our students up to the point of near-violence. Her description is perfectly accurate, I can attest, as an eyewitness.

But my own story will be alone in this volume in that it has a happy ending, because I work with the science students now. In every class, there are a few incandescently-angry leftists. We have far more students who are vaguely liberal for the same reason that young people are liberal everywhere: because they do not yet pay much in taxes. In their papers, and speaking to me, they will even drift into conservative positions because their religious beliefs lead them there, or because they are simply unaware that they are entertaining heresy.

And their instructor is not out to stop them. When I had been marketing myself as a phony leftist, I had been cynical and manipulative. I held my own work in such low esteem that I could prostitute myself and laugh it off. It left a bad taste in my mouth, however. Our new department, and my new science students, offered a chance to make up for the past, and to do so by simply being honest and fair.

Every quarter, I have therefore made a little speech as we begin writing our first paper. You will have noticed, I tell the students, the leftist bias among humanities professors. You will also have noticed that you get a higher grade if you pretend to agree with the professor. I regard that as an obnoxious abuse of power. Your religious and political convictions are none of my business, and you are too old for me to change them anyway. You do not have to pretend to be little communists to get a decent grade. Say what you think.

They do not react with surprise or distaste. A number do not react at all, because they already knew of my odd ways from Rate-My-Professors-dot-com, and signed up specifically to benefit. Among most of the rest, I can see the pleasure, and can almost hear them breathing out in pure relief.

Last quarter, we had trouble with the plumbing in our department building, and they had to tear apart one of my office walls to fix it. I used the occasion to redecorate. At the same time, my wife's HMO gave her a coffee mug with the HMO's name on it, and we already have plenty. I took the mug into the class for the pre-meds. The class is equipped to project images from a computer on the instructor's desk, and I projected a Wikipedia image of the flag of the Republic of Vietnam. That is the yellow flag with three red stripes that was the flag of the anticommunist south, extinguished by the Stalinist north in 1975.

"Quite a few of you know what this is," I announced. On any 25-student UC Davis writing-class roster, five or six names will be resoundingly Vietnamese, and most of their parents or grandparents were boat people, political refugees from the repression imposed by Hanoi. "A lot of your older relatives have plenty of these flags. I'll trade this coffee mug for anyone who can come up with one. I want to put it up in my office, kind of as a symbol of my refusal to make you pretend to be radical leftists. I also want to see if any of the commies in the department know what it is."

The students were delighted, and one produced a flag soon after. It hangs in my office, where it has so far been recognized for what it is only by the Vietnamese students.

From my point of view, admittedly privileged, the situation is not hopeless. Being scientists, and good ones, nearly all of my students are at least open to the claims of reality, just as I learned to be that late evening when I turned on *Nightline*, expecting disaster. I instead saw video of Soviet T-62s burning in the Iraqi desert while the US Army main battle tanks and Bradley Fighting Vehicles pounded onward through the smoke. Ideology is a potent thing, but ultimately, reality has a vote.

"C" for Conservatism, the New Scarlet Letter

Brian E. Birdnow

I will state for the record that I am a conservative. I am not shy about this, nor do I shrink from "labels." I am a trained historian who believes that the role of modern liberalism has been largely harmful, and occasionally disastrous. As a historian, I am able to credit the liberals for the good things they have done, but as a conservative I do believe that we have been on the right side more often than they. I entered my doctoral studies in 1995 with a fully formed conservative worldview and knew that I would encounter mostly liberals along the way. In some respects I welcomed this as a healthy form of exercise, in the sense that I would keep my mind sharp by sparring freely and good-naturedly with those who did not share my views. Still, though, I was haunted by a strange fear that I might be making a big mistake.

What kind of a mistake could I have been making? After all, what seems like a better career plan than earning a doctorate, a terminal degree, in a legitimate field? First of all there exists in academia a certain ethos that squeezes the life out of very interesting material and renders it painfully dull. History is great fun, but seen as a subject of academic inquiry, can become lifeless and turgid in the hands of the liberal professoriate. I rationalized this concern away by telling myself that I could bring some genuine enthusiasm and verve to the lecture hall and the seminar room.

The second cause for concern turned out to be well founded. I worried about the long-term future, particularly as a conservative academic facing hostility in the job market. I subscribed to conservative magazines like *Campus,* the flagship publication of the Intercollegiate Studies Institute, which documented the difficulties conservative academics encounter in the job market. The general decline in the level of civil discourse in academia had been well established by the likes of Allan Bloom in his *Closing of the American Mind* back in 1987 and his thesis had been affirmed by Charles Sykes and others in the early 1990s. (See *Profscam* and *The Hollow Men*, for starters.)

One further reason to seriously ponder the wisdom of pursuing a terminal degree back in the day was the general state of the academic job market in 1995. The market, at least in the Humanities, was fully glutted at that time. Many of the departments were overstocked with aging baby boomers, many of whom had dodged the draft by pursuing graduate studies in the late 1960s and early 1970s. Those folks spent a couple of decades in school, finally earned their doctorates, and immediately stepped into tenure-track positions. By the mid-1990s they were Departmental Chairs and Deans, at the peak of their professional careers. They were in no hurry to retire, and in most cases, they are still around today. In addition to longevity (leading to few new openings) these tenured professors remembered their "enemies," namely the establishment moderate professors of an earlier generation, and determined that now they would hire only those who shared a far leftwing social, cultural, and political orientation. They actively sought out women and minorities who shared their views. Conservative and moderate women and nearly all men were strictly "out" by the mid 1990s.

Since hope springs eternal in the human breast, I disregarded dark clouds and blithely began doctoral studies in late August of 1995. My goal was to complete the degree as quickly as possible, and I rapidly moved through the program. A doctoral program resembles a carnival shooting gallery, wherein a candidate must shoot the targets as they pop up. One need not hit the bullseye every time, but one must avoid a complete miss, if at all possible. I tackled the course work and the seminar papers, the conference presentations, and the first tentative forays into academic publishing. I dealt with many, many difficult people during those years: the intellectually arrogant and overbearing types, the brilliant folks who lived entirely within their own minds and seemed uncomfortable with people, the maddeningly vague types with whom a conversation settled nothing, and the uber-feminists who used every weapon in their arsenal to ruin any male less "sensitive" than Alan Alda. I tallied all of this up as a largely beneficial immersion in the human comedy.

I passed the doctoral exams with distinction in early June of 1997 and began dissertation research while teaching as an Adjunct Professor at Saint Louis University in the summer and fall of 1997. During the '97-'98 academic year I refined my dissertation topic, which was a critical study of the Communist Party in Missouri during the post- World War II period. I began the archival research in earnest in 1998, visiting the Truman and Eisenhower Presidential libraries and the National Archives in Washington. Finally, by the beginning of 1999, I was ready to write, and that is exactly what I did for a full year, finishing the first draft a week before Christmas. I spent the first seven weeks of calendar year 2000 rewriting the manuscript, and submitted a finished copy on February 25th. I defended the dissertation on March 30, 2000, during the Organization of American Historians annual meeting, which was being held on the Saint Louis University campus. My faculty adviser and the dissertation readers welcomed me, informally, to the exclusive fraternity of "Doctors of History" on that afternoon and the degree was formally awarded on May 18, 2000.

Up to this point in my academic career, such as it was, I had met up with liberalism, although, with certain exceptions, it had been relatively benign, and not potentially damaging to one's future. That all changed when I submitted a rewritten copy of the doctoral dissertation for publication. After discussing some of the particulars with friends and mentors I rewrote the work for a wider, popular audience in late 2000 and early 2001. I researched the academic presses and, after due consideration, I sent the completed manuscript to the University of Illinois Press, after a long telephone conversation with their chief editor in the spring of 2001. I sent the work via certified mail on a Monday morning and called the editor on Wednesday afternoon to check on delivery. He told me that it had arrived the previous day, but that he had already return mailed it to me. When I asked why he simply stated that "...I suspect that our prospective readers would disagree with your conclusions," and he refused to elaborate on the remark. The point of view that rendered my conclusions suspect was the belief that CPUSA actually meant no good will and caused the country trouble in the late 1940s and early 1950s. Obviously liberal historians were at work here trying to spike a work critical of the influence of the Communist Party-USA, Missouri branch.

Undaunted, I submitted the work to other presses. The Missouri Historical Society liked the monograph, but decided that it was better suited to an academic press, rather than a popular one. When I returned to the academic presses the response became formulaic. The editors would submit the work to a reader who would respond favorably. They would then submit it to a second reader who would savage the manuscript (and the author) in bitter, personal, abusive and vitriolic terms. This pattern repeated itself with Southern Illinois University Press, Kansas University Press, and University of Missouri Press. The editors, each of whom had told me that they personally liked the work, refused to buck the decision of the critical reader. So, each new adventure ended identically with an editor and a reader responding favorably to the work, while one critical liberal spiked the entire project. I shed no tears for the likes of Bill Maher and Keith Olberman crying about "conservative censorship," since I have experienced the reality of the conspiracy of silence. I finally managed to get the book published by Edwin Mellen Press in 2005.

The dissertation publishing difficulties paled in comparison to those associated with landing a fulltime position. I was fully aware of the decks being stacked against conservative professors/historians but I had earned a doctorate at a very respected institution with American political history as a primary area of concentration. I expected to beat the bushes for a while, but certainly expected to find a position with some future although it may not have been exactly a plum assignment. I had been teaching as an adjunct at Saint Louis University and at St. Louis College of Pharmacy while completing doctoral studies and I stepped onto the adjunct treadmill in earnest in the Fall of 2000. I resumed teaching at the two institutions I mentioned earlier and added spots at St. Louis Community College and at Southern Illinois University at Edwardsville, and at a couple of junior colleges in southwestern Illinois. I was told that I would be "first in line" at each of these places for a permanent gig, if I acquitted myself well.

Life ground tediously on while I worked at thankless positions for slave wages. I applied for literally hundreds of jobs across the world, after finding out, to my chagrin, that I wasn't really the "first in line" at any of the places that I was working, even though my classes were overfilled, my student evaluations were outstanding, and my superiors always rated me as very highly qualified. In addition to the unpleasant realization that I would not secure a position at the places where I was working, I found to my shock that the very ground on which the historical profession stood was undergoing a tectonic shift. Most of the academic positions advertised in the traditional joblists after around 1999 called for historians trained in esoterica such as "Women's Studies," "Chicana History," "Borderlands History," and other multicultural studies. These pseudo-historical comic book topics had supplanted true history in the modern American university.

Finally, in the spring of 2007, I happened to be in the right place at the right time, and got what I figured was a great career break. I was teaching at McKendree College, a small liberal arts institution in Lebanon, Illinois, about 25 miles east of St. Louis. I had started at McKendree as an adjunct in 2005. A tenured professor resigned her position unexpectedly on the final day of the Spring 2007 academic term. The university (McKendree, like every two-bit college, was in the process of transiting to university status for purposes of prestige, at the time) needed to fill the position quickly and the Department Chair knew my credentials were in order. He also knew my work, freely admitting that students asked him why I was not allowed to teach more courses each semester.

The university hired me on as an Assistant Professor, on a one-year contract on May 1, 2007. The university grand poobahs told me that, if I performed credibly, the job would be mine on a permanent basis. I was informed, however, by friends on the inside that I shouldn't get too comfortable with the arrangement, since there had been some grumbling within the faculty ranks because of the fact that the university had replaced a woman with a white man. Nevertheless, I threw myself into the position with great zeal. I taught a course load of six classes per semester, instead of the required four courses, thinking that taking on extra duties would prove my value to the university. I served on the all-university committees and attended an interminable number of mind-numbing meetings. I advised my students, mentored the history majors social club, and generally did what an ambitious assistant professor is expected to do.

In accordance with the instructions I received from my Dean I submitted my credential file in October of 2007, in effect re-applying for the job I already held. Since my performance evaluations were uniformly excellent I assumed that I would emerge as a strong candidate for the position. I did experience a momentary pang of concern in January of 2008 when I inadvertently saw internal documents ranking eleven females as the top candidates on a scale, with myself as the twelfth best person. This was certainly unsettling, but I assumed that everything would right itself in the end.

I was stunned and dismayed when I received an e-mail from my Department Chair on March 12, 2008, informing me that I was not on the interview list for my job. Upon cross-examination he assured me that my job performance had been top notch. His exact words were "…everything I have heard has been extremely positive." He could give me no reason for the exclusion except to repeat the mantra, "…we are required to do a nationwide search." No one on the official university search committee would talk to me or comment on the process whereby I lost my position.

As time passed I found that I had lost out to three laughably bad candidates. The only one of the three who had earned a doctorate spent her time writing about the significance of cookbooks. One candidate who had an MA degree was a member of something called the "Feminist Writers Group" and had stapled essays by New Jersey junior high girls together into a booklet. The third finalist was also an MA who wrote about the crisis of American masculinity in the 1950s, and the American Medical Community's response to masturbation between 1870-1920. We don't know whether the medical community was trying to improve the process, or if they succeeded. The historical consensus is uncertain.

Needless to say, some of the university higher-ups were not happy with the poor quality of the "finalists" they brought in for my job. The university president, himself, shot down the recommendation of the search committee and they offered me the job again, once more on a one-year basis. The Liberal Arts division people told me to apply for the job again, for the third time, when the new search began, in the autumn of 2008. I had signed a contract to write a biography of Gerald Ford for the Nova Science Foundation in April of 2008, so I had improved my position. I applied for the job, once again, but without any real expectation that results would change. I was disappointed, but not really surprised, on December 19th when, after returning home from my nursery school daughter's pre-Christmas concert I received an e-mail from my Dean telling me that I was not a candidate for the job. I had no communication from my department on this matter; in fact I never spoke to my Department chair, or the other fulltime person in the department on the matter. I had NO communication, of any kind, with either of these "colleagues" after October of 2008.

The news of my non-renewal spread quickly around the campus. Some of the History majors protested to the Provost who told them that I was being released due to inferior credentials. She claimed that I did not have a doctorate, and this was the reason for my dismissal. I set the record straight on that score immediately. The same group of students protested to the university President, who said that this was a faculty matter, and that his hands were tied. The Student Government Association passed a resolution declaring that I should be retained, and students took up a petition drive on my behalf.

All of these efforts were undertaken to no avail. I was jettisoned from McKendree in early May of 2009, after refusing to accept a demotion to adjunct. The university eventually hired an Oklahoma State Ph.D. whose scholarly output consisted of writing about prostitution in Tulsa. There is no way of determining whether her research included a fieldwork component, or if she enjoyed her work.

I have since been tossed back onto the adjunct slagheap, which I thought I had escaped in 2007. I teach an average of seven classes per semester, and had eight in the Fall 2012 term. These classes and another job that I work on Saturdays allow me to eke out a living, keeping a roof over my head, and food on the table.

So, what can we learn from this sad and whiny tale of woe? It shows that "credentials" of the old-fashioned kind count for nothing in the modern academy. I have written two books, and contributed six chapters of the American Presidential Encyclopedia. I have published six articles in scholarly journals, and reviewed two other articles for publication. I am also a regular contributor to popular journals like Townhall.com. It counts for nothing. I am marked with a scarlet letter "C," with the letter signifying "Conservative." This, like the mark of Cain, causes good, tolerant, fair and judicious liberals to recoil in horror at the mere mention of my existence. I am a non-person in academia, and I am now in exile!

The Creed of Political Correctness

Jack Kerwick

The contemporary American university can be a very lonely place.

If one is an academic who both plies his craft in any of the liberal arts *and* repudiates the reigning leftist orthodoxy—what I will henceforth call simply, *the creed*—that has become entrenched in his discipline, it *promises* to be a lonely place.

I first became acquainted with the American college setting 18 years ago when I enrolled in a local community college. Since then, I have studied and taught philosophy at a diversity of institutions of higher learning in various areas of the country, from schools that are two-year and four-year, to those that are public and private, religious and secular. For all of their differences, these colleges and universities share one common denominator.

Their faculties tend overwhelmingly to endorse the creed.

Admittedly, the extent to which the prevailing leftist ideology refuses to accommodate alternative perspectives varies from institution to institution. This, however, doesn't alter the fact that it *is* leftist ideology that prevails.

Lest I or any other academic "dissident" be accused of promoting hyperbole, hysteria, or sensationalism, the skeptical reader need only select, at random, virtually any liberal arts department in the country and casually stroll through its corridors. The bumper sticker political slogans that adorn its walls and/or its faculty members' office doors will readily attest to what I and an increasing number of others have had to discover through painful experience: *The ideal of the university as a free market place of competing ideas is a fiction.*

And it is a fiction of the first order.

This revelation on my part didn't come full circle until much later on in my career. However, from the time I first became a student at a local community college in my home state of New Jersey, I began learning that unless I sought perpetual disappointment, I would have to disabuse myself of the naïve belief that my professors were committed to the disinterested pursuit of truth and knowledge.

One of my first courses was in English composition. The instructor was the poster child for the 60's generation, an unreconstructed leftist with a ponytail who didn't even remotely pretend to be anything other than he was. He wasn't a bad teacher, much less uncivil. He could even be stimulating. But he and I would regularly spend *class* time arguing over the whole gamut of political issues—from capital punishment and euthanasia, to abortion and the prison system.

I ultimately received a B in his class. It was my first semester and I didn't think much of it at the time. Yet considering that since that juncture I have earned multiple degrees, including a doctoral degree, but have never received more than a handful of B's (the majority of which were in my foreign language courses), in retrospect I often wonder if my first B in college wasn't at least in part a function of my English professor's political prejudices against me.

There is still another reason that has prompted me to reassess this early experience of mine. Years later, upon receiving my master's degree, I was hired to teach philosophy at this same community college. Now that I was a member of the faculty, I got the opportunity to view up close and all too personally just how politically motivated were many of my colleagues. With alarming frequency, they would openly express their disdain for George W. Bush (who was the President at the time), the

Republican Party, and Fox News. One teacher admitted that it took all of the self-control that she could muster to prevent herself from ejecting bodily a student who dared to defend Bush against one of her tirades.

Faculty members wouldn't just talk about their politics, however. During the 2004 presidential election, they would actually wear *pins* in support of their candidate—Democrat, John Kerry. Other political paraphernalia could be seen on the bulletin boards on the walls outside of their offices.

Not incidentally, presiding over all of this was my old English professor who was now the Chair of the Liberal Arts department.

It was while I was closing in on my doctoral degree, though, that I become fully aware of the omnipresence of the creed. It is then that I was delivered once and for all from the illusion that the average academic would separate his or her politics from teaching and scholarship.

That the "disinterested pursuit of truth" to which the academic has traditionally been depicted as being committed will inevitably be compromised by the prejudices of the pursuer is undeniable. As one fellow philosopher once put it, *what* we see depends upon *how* we look. There is no such thing as a (human) intellect that hasn't been shaped in a complex of ways by the contingencies of time and place, history and tradition. This, however, establishes only that, like any other ideal, it can never be perfectly fleshed out in the real world. It does not mean that it is an unworthy ideal, much less a false one.

During my time at graduate school, as I became ever more immersed in the academic world, I learned from fellow students and mentors alike just how mistaken I am on this score.

I had always thought that, whatever their differences, there existed a trans-partisan consensus among the members of the professorial class that the *raison d'etre* of their being was the acquisition and transmission of knowledge. Instead, what I realized is not just that there was no such consensus; worst, this traditional academic ideal is a Euro-centric instrument of racial, gender, and class oppression.

While many notions that originated among intellectuals have long since made their way into the surrounding culture, this specific idea hasn't (as of yet) succeeded in ensconcing itself into the popular consciousness. At least it hasn't impressed itself with this degree of explicitness. Thus, it will doubtless strike the average person as odd—ludicrous, really—to hear that no small number of the most formally educated people on the planet tirelessly argue on behalf of the proposition that to advance the notion that the truth trumps considerations of, say, race, gender, and class, is to advance "racism," "sexism," and "classism."

It is hard to overstate the degree to which this belief pervades the academy. But a casual perusal of your average college catalogue of courses in literature, history, philosophy, or any of the humanities and social sciences can quickly confirm it.

In my own field, philosophy, a random selection of course descriptions from different institutions reveals the extent to which the creed has corrupted the love of wisdom.

For instance, a distinguished *Catholic* institution in the Philadelphia area offers classes like "Philosophy of Women." The course description reads: "Nature and status of women from ancient times to the present, with consideration of the more general context of self-identity; contemporary feminist theories; feminism as a political movement." This, though, isn't the only gender-centered course in its philosophy brochure. There is also "Eco-Feminism," which explores "basic positions in eco-feminism as they relate to the philosophical and religious traditions of the West." And then, of course, there is good old "Feminist Theory."

Alongside these courses in gender instruction is "Marx and Marxism," a course on Marx's "theories of human nature, freedom and history" and "related developments in Marxist thought."

At the secular institution that awarded me my doctorate, there are classes like: "Recent African Political Thought;" "Black Existentialism;" and "Foucault in Africana Thought." There are also such classes on feminist philosophy as "Feminist Epistemology and Philosophy of Science."

None of this is to suggest that those who teach these courses are necessarily bad or unintelligent teachers, much less bad people. It does, however, establish that both the ubiquity of leftist ideology as well as the allegiance that it commands justifies ascribing to it the character of dogma. That is, it justifies describing it as a creed.

What we know, according to the fashionable academic, is determined by race, gender, and class—what one commentator not inappropriately characterized as the new "holy trinity." The concepts of objectivity, impartiality, "color blind" equality, the rule of law, and their corollaries are in reality the inventions of dead, white men. These men were socially and economically "privileged," heterosexual, and mostly Christian. Today, their posterity continues to peddle these concepts in advancing the interests of their group—to the detriment of racial and religious minorities, women, homosexuals, and the poor.

This is what one discovers upon entering the contemporary university. In fact, this is what one can't *but* discover.

The triadic paradigm of race, gender, and class, broaches no competitors.

This is why it is so problematic.

But not only does its monopolistic reach undercut the imagination by preempting the contemplation of intellectual conceptions that the orthodoxy precludes. Its exclusive focus on the most socially divisive of attributes—its unabashed affirmation of "identity politics"—neatly splits the cosmos into two and only two types of people: on the one hand, those white, "privileged," heterosexual Christian men who insist on asserting their will to power under the guise of the rhetoric of "truth," "knowledge," "objectivity," etc., and, on the other, *everyone else.*

This is a particularly troubling phenomenon for a person like me, a white, heterosexual, Christian man who is also a *conservative.* To just so much as question the view that the concepts constitutive of the traditional academic ideal are the function of "racism," "sexism," "classism," and the rest is taken as proof that the objector is guilty of harboring these most egregious of transgressions.

As a philosopher, I confess to being especially disheartened by the ease with which my colleagues have not only acquiesced in, but enthusiastically embraced, the academic status quo. To be clear, it isn't that they have refused to question *this* status quo; it is that they've refused to question *the* status quo — regardless of its content. Yet in so doing, they betray their mission, a mission that Socrates — the quintessential philosopher — illuminated millennia ago when he famously declared that "the unexamined life is not worth living."

Those characteristics that are supposed to distinguish the academic — intellectual curiosity, the disposition to subject the orthodoxy to withering interrogation, not necessarily because one doesn't accept it, but *just because it is the orthodoxy* — are conspicuously absent from much of today's academy. In their stead is a commitment on the part of academics, not to familiarizing students (or themselves) with the civilization that is their inheritance, not to truth or clarity, but to advancing the goals of "social justice."

Today's typical academic is an *activist.* He *or she,* like all true believers in some still distant promised land, is marked by a virtually obsessive focus on the future. It isn't that the past isn't invoked. It is. But when so — and this is no less the case in the field of history than anywhere else — it is meticulously mined for only those events and figures that can be enlisted in the service of present purposes, namely, the purpose of bringing to fruition the future of the activist educator's imaginings.

To put it a bit more bluntly, the past is exploited in order to clear the way for the future.

Another salient characteristic of the contemporary *secular* university that has left me especially struck is the veiled—and not always so veiled—contempt in which academics tend to hold traditional Christianity. This contempt is expressed in various ways, from ill-informed denunciations of Christianity's involvement in the Crusades, slavery, and the Holocaust, to its alleged perpetuation of "patriarchy" and "homophobia." Most tellingly on this score is the state of sheer neglect to which the medieval era—approximately *1,000 years* of Western philosophy—is relegated. To search its course catalog for a single class on any Christian thinker promises to be an exercise in futility.

Lest I be misunderstood, in the interests of fairness, it must be said that for as vast a bastion of leftist ideology that the university has become, there are nonetheless good people there to be found. That is to say, there are some very kind proponents of leftist ideology. There are also some not so congenial folks. However, it should be stressed that, ultimately, individual personalities are not the issue.

The challenges with which dissident professors are compelled to reckon are of a systemic nature.

To put it another way, the nearly impenetrable force that the non-leftist professor is up against is not this or that faculty, but *the creed*. It is a quasi-religious *dogma,* a leftist *orthodoxy,* with which he (or she) must grapple. This makes matters all that much more formidable, for the dogma is like the air that the academic breathes: it is at once invisible and ubiquitous.

Leftist dogma pervades instruction in the classroom, it is true. But it also informs faculty hiring decisions. It isn't just, or even primarily, that faculties are dominated by leftist ideologues with an animus toward those who don't think like them. There need not be any such (at least conscious) animus at all. More importantly, such decisions are made in large measure on the basis of candidates' research interests and publications. But since leftist ideology has long achieved hegemonic status in the academic world, scholarly fashions and fads reflect this fact. Conferences and journals are overwhelmingly centered in the themes of "social" or "global justice" and their variants—"racism," "sexism," "homophobia," etc.

The deck is stacked considerably against those who do not care to explore these topics. It is stacked even more so against those of us who are critical of them.

I am now in my 13th year of teaching philosophy. Every year I wind up teaching anywhere between ten and twelve courses. I remain an adjunct instructor, you see, making ends meet by teaching at three to four schools per semester (including summer terms). Thankfully, I haven't had any difficulties getting hired anywhere. I just haven't been able to secure a permanent position at any one institution.

Whether my challenges stem from my standing as a white, heterosexual, conservative man or just a fiercely competitive field and a bad economy, is uncertain. However, as this essay aimed to make clear, one thing *is* for certain: anyone aspiring to make a living as an academic in today's university is guaranteed to have a tough go at it as long as he or she plans on resisting the leftist ideology that is its creed.

Afterword: The Formulated Phrase

Mary Grabar

The eyes that fix you in a formulated phrase...

T. S. Eliot, "The Love Song of J. Alfred Prufock"

No doubt the counterarguments will be coming, as they have any time a conservative professor claims discrimination. The bar for proof will be raised high. First, will be the charge that these are all "anecdotal" examples of academic discrimination. They do not form a scientific study. We cannot know if the individuals writing here had other reasons for not attaining full employment or social acceptance. There is no *proof* of discrimination. They may not be good scholars. Or a "good fit" for the needs of the college. And on and on.

Such excuses always come, despite the fact that surveys confirm what conservative and moderate academics already know from firsthand experience. These surveys come out regularly, and just as regularly, and predictably, leftist professors come out with ways to explain away the discrimination. The end result is a self-satisfied ruling class of leftist academics who continue business as usual.

To see how this is done, let's look at the release of a recent survey. The one by the University of California at Los Angeles Education Research Institute is conducted every three years, with the latest one in October 2012. It showed that nationally "professors, already liberal, have moved further to the left." That is how the headline of the October 24, 2012, *Inside Higher Ed* article[1] put it. Middle of the road and conservative professors are increasingly being crowded out by liberals and those on the far left. Since the 1998-9 survey, the percentage identifying as liberal or far left increased from 47.5 percent to 62.7 percent. The survey also showed that younger faculty tend to be increasingly liberal or far left, thus portending an even greater imbalance in the future, as M.D. Allen illustrated so well. But the director of the Institute, Sylvia Hurtado, when asked by the reporter, sidestepped the issue by theorizing that as older, more conservative professors retire they are replaced by increasingly leftist younger professors. (Interestingly, the same survey showed that community college professors tend to be more conservative than those at the more prestigious four-year schools and research universities. No mention was made of possible discrimination when conservatives are relegated to community colleges where they have larger teaching loads, less pay and prestige, and very little opportunity to disseminate their ideas through conferences, publications, or media appearances.)

Another way to explain away discrimination is through studies that seem to pop up on as perennial a basis as tulips. One of the most discussed of these studies has been "Why are professors liberal?"[2] by University of British Columbia sociology professor Neil Gross and Harvard University graduate student Ethan Fosse. Gross, a self-admitted non-conservate, concludes that rather than outright hostility and discrimination, the conservative academic is faced with a culture that is alien to him. Personality factors, like religious belief and values, explain why conservatives are underrepresented, according to the study's authors. The American academy began drifting leftward when it abandoned its seminarian roots in the nineteenth century. So it's only natural that the religious conservative would increasingly find an academic atmosphere at odds with his faith-based worldview. Additionally, conservatives tend to have larger families and to be more concerned with making money. Overall, it's just not a good fit for the academic life.

Afterword: The Formulated Phrase

Gross and Fosse conclude,

> We found that professors are more liberal than other Americans because a higher proportion have advanced credentials, exhibit a disparity between their levels of education and income [i.e., make less money], have distinctive religious profiles [are Jewish or secular], and express tolerance for controversial ideas.

They admit that this argument is circular and concede that political correctness is (also) marked by intolerance. Yet, such an observation cannot *explain* the lack of conservatives in the academy.

They present a theory:

> Our theory . . . holds that the liberalism of professors, at least in the contemporary American context, is a function . . . of the systematic sorting of young adults who are already liberally- or conservatively-inclined into and out of the academic profession, respectively.

Gross and Fosse are correct about the "sorting," although they underplay it greatly. Similarly, Sylvia Hurtado, the director of the Higher Education Research Institute, dismissed concerns about the increasing political imbalance among the professoriate shown by the October 2012 survey. She contended that the leftward shift did not impact professors' teaching or treatment of students. The *Inside Higher Ed* article noted her reference to "a series of studies showing no evidence that left-leaning faculty members are somehow shifting the views of their students or enforcing any kind of political requirement."

This is either conscious or unconscious denial. (The "series of studies" was based on self-reporting by the faculty members.) The stories from our campuses tell us that professors tend to impose their leftwing worldviews on students and often punish students who openly challenge them. This is now common knowledge. Apologists for the status quo like Gross and Hurtado gloss over incidents of outright hostility by tenured faculty members against dissenting students at the undergraduate and graduate level. (Another volume of essays needs to be compiled of students who were dissuaded from pursuing academic careers.)

Few young adults will make waves when it comes to their grades. As a college instructor, I know that most simply want to do what is expected to get a good grade. It is unusual to have a student publicly expose a professor's biased test questions as Zachary Freeman did in a post for the *College Conservative*. Freeman reproduced an exam question he was given as a freshman in Professor John Garrett's economics class during the fall of 2010 at the University of Tennessee, Chattanooga:[3]

> *Question 1: "What caused the financial markets crisis of 2007?"*
>
> *Correct Answer: "Republicans"*
>
> *Question 2: "Why did Bush side with water companies who contaminated water with arsenic?"*
>
> *A: Bush heard that arsenic caused kidney stones in cats and he didn't like cats.*
>
> *B: Because people said 'Don't Mess With Texas' and it's enough of a mess already.*
>
> *C: (and the correct answer) Because he was in favor of deregulation and always gave executives what they wanted.*

Why would a student like Zachary Freeman even think about a career in academia? Certainly, he would not be able to turn to Professor Garrett for guidance or encouragement. Most of the students in Professor Garrett's class probably gave the answer he wanted—either happy to confirm such prejudices or just cynical about higher learning.

I've witnessed such hostility when the president of the AAUP dismissed a student's catalogue of examples of bias as "that's your testimony" in a public forum. I've heard numerous stories from my own students about biased professors.

In the summer of 2011 when I was a Bakwin Research Fellow studying George S. Schuyler at the Alexander Hamilton Institute for the Study of Western Civilization, I met Hamilton College students there seeking intellectual stimulation and support for serious scholarship. The faculty at Hamilton College had famously forced the independently funded Institute off campus, after illegally attempting to take control of it.[4] Robert Paquette and the few other Hamilton faculty who set up the Institute offer students classes, lectures, conferences, and work study programs there. One young man who had won academic awards and had a promising future as a professor of classics and mathematics changed his major to finance after being discriminated against by his professors. For example, this student was told by a professor that only backwards people, like Fox News viewers, read Plato's *Republic*. Translation exercises were to include analogies to the "terroristic" war policies of President George W. Bush. This made a hostile learning environment for him.

In Neil Gross and Ethan Fosse's scheme, though, this student's decision then to pursue a career in finance would be put into the nebulous category of a bad political/cultural fit. But the reality is much different. Students complained to me that their professors did not even teach the subject matter—the classics or history or English—but used the classes to promote their political agenda. In order to succeed in academia, where professors advance through the judgment of their peers, such students knew that they would have to do the same thing. Gross and Fosse minimize the hostility not only to conservative students, but to traditional scholarship, on our campuses. Such professors not only dissuade students from academic careers but from completing college. They punish students through grades, sometimes refusing to return papers. So a student's decision to pursue a career on Wall Street should not be taken as evidence that conservatives are more concerned with making money than scholarship.

When we consider the stories from the contributors to this volume and from students, we can see how intimidating the academic environment can be to conservatives these days. Yet, sociologists minimize the hostility. Gross and Fosse claim,

> Our theory also has implications for the controversy over 'liberal bias' in higher education. On one side, our theory challenges the assumption of some conservative critics that rampant discrimination against conservatives in hiring and promotion is the main cause of the liberal tilt of the faculty. Some such discrimination may occur—it is not difficult to find professors who freely admit they would be uncomfortable voting to hire a conservative colleague—and we have built tacit judgments of political fit into our theoretical model.

The scare quotes surrounding "liberal bias" suggest that it is imaginary. The term "assumption" before "rampant discrimination" makes it sound unreasonable. The combination of qualifiers and word choice throw into doubt the idea that conservatives face discrimination. Of *course* one can always find those who would be "uncomfortable voting to hire a conservative colleague," imply Gross and Fosse. One can *always* find exceptions, but scientists know that exceptions do not *prove* anything. There is no hostility: such professors are merely "uncomfortable." If you look hard enough you can find disgruntled employees who don't fit in with the culture anywhere ("it is not difficult to find"). Rather than actually talking to discriminated-against professors, the sociologists dismiss the idea of "explicit discrimination." They say so in the next sentence: "our theory is capable of accounting for the general tendency of professors to be liberal without making recourse to explicit discrimination."

What they don't say is that the army of attorneys at each institution makes *sure* there *is* no "*explicit* discrimination."

The question—that would be investigated in detail were the underrepresentation in an approved ethnic or gender group—is dismissed. (A small industry of studies is supported for explaining the underrepresentation of women, minorities, gays, etc.) Finally, these sociologists ignore the fact that conservatives would have no problem with liberal colleagues were liberal politics not a precondition for employment or for doing scholarship.

To their credit, Gross and Fosse dispense with the scurrilous, unsupported theory of the "authoritarian personality," put out by the academics of the Marxist Frankfurt School in 1950 that attempted to tie conservatism to fascism. They also dispute the idea that "professors tend to be liberal because liberals are smarter than conservatives" and theorize,

> American society is selecting professors not on the basis of intelligence or insight alone, but rather on the basis of a conjunction of perceived academic potential and liberal politics—a development long in the making that might, depending on one's point of view, be seen as having positive or negative consequences for scientific and scholarly creativity.

What Gross and Fosse present is a benign, almost unconscious, discrimination. If there is a bias, it is toward a more liberal (open) view. It furthermore may even have "positive consequences for scientific and scholarly creativity."

In the previously cited *Inside Higher Ed* article, Gross remarked that the shift leftward, even towards radicalism, probably arose from a concern about inequality during a time of economic downturn: "'From the vantage point of some folks, that will make academe look bad. For others, it will make academe look like a place concerned with the country.'" He gives leftist professors the benefit of the doubt, and even suggests patriotic motives. It never seems to occur to Gross that a healthy testing of ideas is more likely to lead to more creativity. Nor that the period of extreme radicalism, the 1960s, when the assault on universities began, was a period of economic prosperity.

Gross and Fosse avoid the heart of the matter because they do not take note of how much scholarship is now confused with left-wing ideology. Scholarship is now the handmaiden to politics, with entire departments set up to advance political interests, like departments of "labor studies" or those like the Department of Critical Culture, Gender and Race Studies at Washington State University. In my field of literary studies, to insist—in a conservative manner—on a respectful approach to the old literary masters of the West is the kiss of death on the job market. One is *required* to scour literature for evidence of the sins of imperialism, sexism, classicism, racism, etc. It is the same in other fields. As we've seen, one cannot even point to the real practices of Islam because to do so goes against the prevailing anti-Western creed. As Martin Slann discovered, reality does not interfere; a reference to facts will excommunicate one from his colleagues. To criticize the kind of scholarship that the feminists who competed with Brian Birdnow engaged in is to challenge the prevailing notion that the study of history should serve the feminist agenda. To do these things is considered apostasy by the new priestly class of academics.

But if the new elite class of academics won't allow conservatives and moderates to join their ranks as equals, they do use them as objects of study in order to advance their peculiar form of scholarship. Tellingly, shortly before the publication of the "Why are professors liberal?" study, Gross, along with Thomas Medvetz, of University of California-San Diego, and Rupert Russell, of Harvard University, published a study in the *Annual Review of Sociology* titled "The Contemporary American Conservative Movement,"[5] where they noted, "The political valences of numerous occupations reflect self-selection based on perceptions of fit with liberal or conservative self-identity more than objective economic interests." In other words, people choose professions for reasons other than economics, like values and aptitudes. Conservatives tend to go into professions like police work and engineering instead of the artistic or scholarly fields.

The sociologists note the rise in number of Republicans who describe themselves as conservative, from 43 percent in 1976 to 66 percent in 1996, and recommend that sociologists "devote more attention to the mainstream American conservative movement." Such studies could provide insight on "the sociology of intellectuals, theoretical work on social change, and research on social stratification."

 They claim that sociologists have mistakenly avoided studying conservatism because they have failed to see its historical meaning, because of a lack of interest in conventional politics, and because they hold stereotypical views: "conservative movements are regarded as having altogether different properties and characteristics from their counterparts on the left (which at its worst moments yields simplistic depictions of conservatism as a conspiracy of the powerful or a confederacy of dunces)." Finally, there is "a disinclination on the part of sociologists to study individuals and groups toward whom they are not personally sympathetic."

All these assumptions—especially the last one—presuppose that sociology is a field only for liberals. Conservatism for sociologists is an object of "historical" and political *study*—and therefore not a personally held worldview. Sociologists are unable to see the similarities with the left—the benchmark. Sociologists are not sympathetic to conservatives because they themselves are not conservative. Gross and company are not speaking to *conservative* sociologists, as few as there are. The "self-selection" that they see dominating academia, ironically, infects their own field to the point where they can't see it.

Rather, they see conservatism as a kind of exotic intellectual development that can be studied from their — liberal — perspective. While to their credit they acknowledge that too often their colleagues present conservatives unfairly as a "confederacy of dunces," they nonetheless present conservatism not as an at least equally legitimate worldview in which to *engage* with *colleagues,* but as a phenomenon to be studied from an intellectually superior, ostensibly scientific, perch.

Social science literature is filled with cautions about making cultural assumptions for practices ranging from ear lobe extensions to cannibalism. But here the sociologists presume to study conservatives. Conservatives under the microscope, in spite of the lip service, are presented as — to use the language of the left — the "other."

Indeed, there are now centers for the *study* of conservatism and these display the worst aspects of the sociologists' perspective. One is the insultingly named Berkeley Center for Right-Wing Studies.[6] One of the two visiting scholars in residence, Ruth Rosen, writes for the George Soros-supported sites *AlterNet* and *openDemocracy*. Her articles include "'Drugged by Testosterone': Why Did Bill Keller and Other Male Pundits Support the Iraq War?" and "Women are the key to presidential debate and election." The Center provides support to graduate students writing dissertations on aspects of fascism in Mussolini's African empire and in movements in Eastern Europe — along with studies on the Tea Party. Yes, fascist dictator Mussolini and the Tea Party are lumped together into the category of "Right-Wing Studies."

After hosting a conference on the Tea Party in fall 2010, the Center published a collection of related essays by participants

Afterword: The Formulated Phrase

in August 2012, *Steep: The Precipitous Rise of the Tea Party*. We already get an idea about what these supposedly academic essays will be like by the first chapter, "The Tea Party in Historical Perspective: A Conservative Response to a Crisis of Political Economy." Author Charles Postel of San Francisco State University, under the veneer of historical overview, gives away his prejudices when he claims that the "right-wing rage" of the Tea Party is irrational (because it seeks the free market solutions that he claims led to the 2008 recession), embodies the concerns of older, white Americans (who have racism lurking in their hearts), and shares similarities to the Cold War era of "apocalyptic fears of communism" which were exploited by the John Birch Society and other corporate conservative groups (today "corporate foundations" and Fox News). Postel taps into all the stereotypes about the Tea Party, including subliminal racism. For sources, he relies on left-wing popular media as well as academic sources.

Interestingly, Postell ignores the one poll that gathered demographic information about the Tea Party. It was conducted by the *New York Times* and published in April 2010 — in perfect timing for the Tea Party conference that fall — had they chosen to use it. The poll refuted the stereotypes that the media was already spreading. It found that contrary to depictions, most Tea Party members had higher incomes and were better-educated than the general public.[7] The *New York Times* article[8] about it noted, "Their responses are like the general public's in many ways," with most Tea Party members describing the amount they paid in taxes as "fair," most sending their children to public schools, most claiming that Sarah Palin was not qualified to be president, and most believing that Social Security and Medicare are worth the cost to taxpayers. The three main concerns of Tea Party members were "the recent health care overhaul, government spending and a feeling that their opinions are not represented in Washington" — hardly the concerns of wild-eyed latter-day John Birchers. Yet, despite the mainstream views, the *New*

York Times reporters chose to close the article by quoting Tea Party members who would give the opposite impression to *New York Times* readers, with one predicting an ominous-sounding "revolt" to stop excessive spending and one claiming Obama to be a socialist.

In general, the Tea Party is made up of the kind of demographic that is widely respected. These are successful, educated people who are politically informed. This poll, however, was quickly forgotten, and journalists and academics instead referred to unsubstantiated examples of racism and sought out individuals who are not representative or were agents provocateurs.[9] The essays in the collection published by the Center for Right-Wing Studies continue the stereotypes with such titles: "Reframing Populist Resentments in the Tea Party Movement," "The Tea Party: A 'White Citizenship' Movement?" and "Grand Old Tea Party: Partisan Polarization and the Rise of the Tea Party Movement." The last one is by political science professor Alan Abramowitz, whom I heard speak about his new book, *The Polarized Public: Why American Government Is So Dysfunctional*, at a 2012 Labor Day weekend book festival.

Polarization, declared Professor Abramowitz to the Obama-festooned, overwhelmingly white audience, is at a level not seen in 100 years. The divides, racially, ideologically, and culturally, have grown. For evidence of the racial divide, he presented a Power Point slide of an Obama rally that showed a good number of black people. The Romney rally was all white. Abramowitz heralded the change in demographics due to immigration and birth rates that would lead to a Democratic victory in November.

The polarization, he explained, is due to increased party loyalty, with fewer marginal House districts, fewer battleground states, and more campaign focus on mobilization of the base. This is happening among both parties, said Abramowitz, but it is the Republican Party that has swung the most from the center.

Afterword: The Formulated Phrase

One could have predicted the examples of polarizing figures he showed: the Tea Party, Fox News, Sarah Palin, and Glenn Beck (the latter paired with Father Coughlin). The professor did not mention the *New York Times* poll. Instead, he made in-jokes of the kind I've heard at academic conferences. He had begun his talk by stating that he forgot to bring an empty chair, a reference to Republican National Convention speaker Clint Eastwood. To illustrate polarity, he showed a slide of signs showing Obama depicted as both a communist and national socialist. He also showed one of Bush with a Hitler mustache. While both were presented as examples of extremism, he joked that the latter was "true." I've been to several Tea Party rallies and have not seen any signs comparing Obama to Hitler or Stalin. Black Tea Party members were always warmly welcomed. But Abramowitz made no mention of actually attending events or talking to Tea Party activists.

He simply blamed Republicans, like Newt Gingrich. He noted that not one Republican voted for the Obama health care bill (no mention made of how Republicans were excluded). Since the 2010 elections, when Republicans won back the House, there has been no cooperation between the parties, he claimed. Conservatives tend to see liberals as the "enemy," and so on. In short, the "study" of polarization was an exercise in further polarization through stereotyping and blame.

Similarly, Abramowitz's fellow scholars at the Center for Right-Wing studies demonize conservatives. "Studies" of "right-wing movements" are intended to confirm the biases of left-wing professors, clearly, and furthermore with the support of taxpayers who pay for the California university system. The demand is over and over to accept their creed and proceed from there.

So, we have it by their own admission: Whether by the careful wording of Gross and company or the aspersions of fascism cast upon the Tea Party by "scholars" at the Center for Right-

103

Wing Studies, conservative ideas are deemed not worthy of serious investigation or engagement.

When creed prevails, conversations become Inquisitions. Those who do not adhere to the creed are declared racists, sexists, fascists, etc. While the left repeats that they are the standard-bearers for racial tolerance, they do not allow for the person who is of color to disagree. Abramowitz, in his presentation, ignored black and Hispanic keynote speakers at the Republican convention, and instead presented selective pictures of rallies and ridiculed Clint Eastwood. This creed has been adopted from the communists of the 1920s, who claimed that capitalism by its nature is racist and who put out propaganda that communism was the cure for racism.

The December 18, 2012, op-ed in the *New York Times* by University of Pennsylvania professor of political science Adolph L. Reed, Jr., on the nomination by South Carolina Governor Nikki Haley of Congressman Tim Scott to the Senate to replace Jim DeMint, continues in the same vein. Reed presumes to read the mind and motivations of both Haley (of Indian origin) and Scott (of American-American origin).

The fact that Scott will be the first black senator from the South since Reconstruction, the first black Republican senator since 1979, and only the seventh African-American ever to serve in the chamber, to Reed, is merely "racial symbolism" that "plays to the Republicans' desperate need to woo (or at least appear to woo) minority voters." Professor Reed continues, and repeats an unsubstantiated trope about the racism of the Tea Party: "Even if the Republicans managed to distance themselves from the thinly veiled racism of the Tea Party adherents who have moved the party rightward, they wouldn't do much better among black voters than they do now." Reed "suspects that appointments like Mr. Scott's are directed less at blacks. . . than at whites who are inclined to vote Republican but don't want to have to think of themselves, or be thought of by others, as racist." Of course, the same suspicions are not applied to whites who are Democrats. Such projection of "thinly veiled" racism is decidedly unscholarly.

Reed predicts that Scott would not win the election in 2014. He concludes, "Republicans will not gain significant black support unless they take policy positions that advance black interests. No number of Tim Scotts—or other cynical tokens—will change that." Of course, suggesting that Scott is a "token" not only implies that Republicans can't be genuinely accepting of blacks, but that Scott allows himself to be used or is incapable of understanding what the Republican Party stands for.

Reed's argument furthermore is tautological: "Black interests" are synonymous with the Democrat agenda; therefore, in order to advance "black interests" one must be a Democrat. Reed illustrates the kind of thinking displayed by the liberal sociologists studying conservatives and by the academics studying the Tea Party at the Center for Right-Wing Studies. Conclusions are predetermined. In a most unscholarly manner, no effort is made to consider ideas or evidence outside of the dominant ideology—for example that economic independence, family and religious values, or Constitutional law can advance black interests. Evidence about the exploitation of blacks by communists and the New Left or the devastating effects of progressive policies, and from conservative black intellectuals themselves—like George Schuyler, Joseph H. Jackson, Homer Smith, Star Parker, or Thomas Sowell—are simply ignored, or dismissed as "tokenism." And it is not only blacks who are defined this way. When John McCain nominated Alaska Governor Sarah Palin as his running mate in 2008, feminists like Gloria Steinem contended that Palin could not have women's interests at heart.

For Reed only the Democrat Party (that is increasingly redistributive) can cure racism. For Steinem, and feminist professors who hate Palin with a passion, only a pro-choice Democrat woman can cure sexism. It's only a redistributive agenda that can cure social ills; arguments and evidence to the contrary are simply dismissed.

In short, Reed does what most academics do these days, and that is demand that the other side accept his ideology. He says as much when he claims that Republicans must change their "policy positions" in order to "advance black interests." In other words, Republicans must become Democrats.

This is academia writ large upon our political canvas. The one-party rule in academia trickles down to the political arena. For all their scientific pretensions (they say liberals are more open to science because they are not as religious), political scientists like Reed and Abramowitz do not bother to collect *evidence* of racism within the Tea Party or the Republican Party, but simply take liberties in interpretation and charge conservatives with "thinly veiled racism." They simply ignore studies, polls, and historical evidence. They ignore the voices of dissenters—even if they are from the groups whose "interests" they claim to have at heart.

We can expect that Professor Reed's statements will not be challenged in the academy by the historical evidence and current political realities. Now in complete power in the academy, Reed and his like-minded colleagues wipe contrary evidence off the syllabi, ignore it in their scholarship, and neglect to preserve and archive it. They become the public voices of the academy, enjoying the full prestige of their titles and positions.

The academy is still the institution where ideas are given the imprimatur of respectability, and those who reside there are granted respectability too. But such respect is often undeserved. Those now in power have been unable or unwilling to defend their ideas legitimately. They have resorted to illegitimate methods to defend their turf. They have used their power of numbers. We know by the first-hand stories that the academic regime today is illegitimate because it can deal with dissenters only by sending them into exile.

[1] Jaschik, Scott. "Survey finds that professors, already liberal, have moved further to the left." *Inside Higher Ed.* October 24, 2012.

http://www.insidehighered.com/news/2012/10/24/survey-finds-professors-already-liberal-have-moved-further-left

[2] *Theory and Society: Renewal and Critique in Social Theory.* Springer Science + Business Media B.V. 2012, published online January 29, 2012.

[3] Freeman, Zachary. College Conservative, December 14, 2011.

[4] Paquette, Robert. "What Happened at Hamilton." *Minding the Campus.* September 27, 2007.

http://www.mindingthecampus.com/originals/2007/09/centerbuilding_at_hamilton_col.html

[5] Gross, Neil, Thomas Medvetz, and Rupert Russell. "The Contemporary American Conservative Movement." *Annual Review of Sociology.* Volume 37. August 2011. 37:325-54.

[6] Berkeley Center for Right-Wing Studies

http://crws.berkeley.edu/

[7] Zernike, Kate and Megan Thee-Brenan. "Poll Finds Tea Party Backers Wealthier and More Educated." *New York Times.* April 14, 2010

http://www.nytimes.com/2010/04/15/us/politics/15poll.html

[8] *Ibid.*

[9] Kincaid, Cliff. "Agents Provocateurs and the Tea Parties." *Accuracy in Media.* April 14, 2010.

http://www.aim.org/aim-report/agents-provocateurs-and-the-tea-parties/

Contributors

M. D. Allen is Professor of English at the University of Wisconsin-Fox Valley, where he has taught for more than twenty years. He has been openly conservative for about fifteen years. The main focus of Allen's research is late Victorian English novelist George Gissing, especially Gissing's interest in French literature and its influence on his own writings.

Brian Birdnow is a historian, teacher, essayist, and security officer, although not necessarily in that order. He is the author of *Communism, Anti-Communism, and the Federal Courts in Missouri: 1952-1958* and *Gerald R. Ford: The All-American President.* He is the co-author, along with the Dissident Prof herself, of *"A New Beginning," Or a Revised Past? President Barack Obama's Cairo Speech.*

Mary Grabar received her Ph.D. in English from the University of Georgia in 2002, and has since then taught in a number of colleges and universities in Georgia. She writes frequently about education and culture for such publications as the *Weekly Standard, Minding the Campus, PJ Media, Roll Call, Accuracy in Media, Front Page Magazine,* and others. She started Dissident Prof in 2011.

Scott Herring teaches writing and literature at the University of California, Davis. Before he got his Ph.D., he worked for years in Yellowstone National Park; he still carries on a hopeless love affair with the place, and has written about it in a wide range of publications. Having learned, from researchers working in Greater Yellowstone, something of how a variety of sciences work, he has the privilege of teaching mainly the advanced science students at his campus.

Dr. Paul Kengor is professor of political science at Grove City College. He is a New York Times bestselling author whose books include *The Crusader: Ronald Reagan and the Fall of Communism, Dupes: How America's Adversaries Have Manipulated Progressives for a Century*, and (most recently) *The Communist: Frank Marshall Davis, The Untold Story of Barack Obama's Mentor*.

Jack Kerwick has a bachelor's degree in philosophy and religion from Wingate University, a master's degree in philosophy from Baylor University, and a doctoral degree in philosophy from Temple University. His areas of specialization are ethics and political philosophy, and his research interests lie in the study of classical conservative thought. He teaches at a variety of colleges in New Jersey and Pennsylvania.

Martin Slann received his doctorate in Political Science from The University of Georgia. He is the author, co-author, and co-editor of several scholarly books and introductory texts. He is Professor of Political Science at The University of Texas at Tyler.